MW00942854

The Brooklyn Kid

by

Domenick Scarlato, Ed.D

The Brooklyn Kid
© 2018 by Domenick Scarlato, Ed.D

All rights reserved. No part of this book may be reproduced in any form or by any means without permission in writing from the author, except for brief quotations in a review.

All photos are the property of the author.

Cover picture by Domenick Scarlato, Ed.D

All rights reserved; not to be used without permission in any commercial publication.

Acknowledgement

I wish to thank my wife, Laraine
For all the patience and assistance
she gave me

All my love –
Heart and Soul

TABLE OF CONTENTS

The Brooklyn Kid is a dramatic story of events
which leads a boy through manhood, only to reach
not a crossroad, but four crossroads.

He could only choose one to follow.

After reading these interesting adventures, which
road would you choose?

ONE - The Kid

Once upon a time, on a dark rainy night, a man named Funzi Divita rode on the Myrtle Avenue "El" train in Brooklyn, New York City. He was a notorious gambler who owed the Shellacs a great deal of money, and he was very late in his payments. He tried to avoid them. Shellacs were hoods who gave loans to poor souls, at an exorbitant rate of interest. If a person did not pay they would break his arm, or worse, kill him.

There were two Shellacs waiting for the train at the foot of the stairs at Franklin Avenue Elevator Train Station.

At the same time a baby was being born at 114 Franklin Avenue, a half a block away from the train station. In 1928, many poor families had their babies delivered at home by a midwife. A midwife was an elderly woman experienced in delivering babies. At the Scarlato's home a kitchen table was used to have Carmela deliver her baby. The table was placed near the kitchen sink so as to have plenty of hot water, and a place to dispose of the waste. Carmela was a very strong woman, and she painfully delivered a ten-pound baby boy named Domenick. He was named after his grandfather and his father, Damiano "Tom" Scarlato, was very proud.

The Elevator train came roaring into Franklin Avenue Station, and the only passenger who got off was Divita. As he descended the stairs he stopped halfway. He spotted two men at the bottom of the stairs, and with that he turned to run back up the stairs. Both men fired a volley shots, hitting Divita many times. Divita came tumbling down, and at the foot of the bloodied stairs died. The two men disappeared into the night. They used to say that when a person dies, a baby is born to take its place. How true!

In 1929, during the historic Stock Market Crash, the Scarlatos moved to 512 Kent Avenue. Though the memories of a five year old are cloudy, Domenick remembers certain incidents. He remembers vividly when his mother, who was pregnant with his brother Salvatore, fell down the long concrete steps in front of their apartment. She had gone outside to retrieve a bottle of milk. She was wearing open back slippers, which caused her fall. The bottle of milk shattered, and the ragged base of the bottle stuck to her elbow. It was a miracle that she survived the fall and that Salvatore was born normal. Domenick always said he would never forget that incident, especially when he saw the scars on his mother's elbow.

Another incident which Domenick said haunts his dreams, is when their dog, Dickey, died. Dickey was a small, curly-haired, pure white ball of fur. He was the cutest dog Domenick ever knew. One evening, Domenick was looking out through a rear window into the backyard, and he saw Dickey jumping around in circles. He called his mother and said, "Mommy, look at Dickey. He's dancing." In reality, Dickey was dying from ingesting rat poison. The rat poison had been planted in the backyard by the landlord. The backyard had open sheds which were rented out to vegetable push-cart vendors. The residue in of vegetables in the carts drew rats. So the landlord planted rat poison. It is too bad he didn't tell Domenick's parents. If he had warned them, Dickey would not have died so horribly.

The third incident which Domenick recalled, happened at Christmas time. It was a beautiful sight to see snow falling beneath a clear full moon. His mother and father called him to look out the backyard window. Looking out, the boy saw Santa Claus walking on the roofs of the open sheds. Santa climbed down to the ground and began walking towards the house. Domenick was so awed that he was speechless. Santa came and knocked on the backdoor! Domenick was petrified, but he responded to Santa's greetings. Santa Claus had a large bag on his back and he asked the boy to help look for his toys. Elated and excited, Domenick stumbled and fell against Santa, causing some of his clothing to tear away. The clothes were not cloth, but rather crepe paper, which caused some tears. Domenick said that he was sorry and told Santa that he was falling apart. Everyone got a good laugh. It is to be noted that Santa Claus was actually Domenick's Uncle Andy, who was married to his mother's sister, Mary.

The toys Domenick pulled from the bag were a milkman's horse and wagon, candy, and a Red Ryder Lever Action B-B gun. The Red Ryder made him jump for joy. Unfortunately, his joy was short lived. When he operated the lever to cock the rifle, he left the lever open. When loading a B-B gun, the lever must be opened and then fully closed. By opening the lever, Domenick compressed a large spring, so when he pulled the trigger the lever closed with tremendous force. His hand was caught between the lever and the pistol grip. He screamed in excruciating pain. It was amazing that his fingers were not broken. His father took the rifle and broke it in half. Even though Domenick was in such pain, he cried more for the rifle than his hand. It is too bad that the adults did not read the instructions that came with the rifle. Although this was a very bad experience for the boy, Domenick never feared firearms. In fact he became a competitive shooter, a hunter, and a collector of firearms. The incident was simply one of many things in life which he overcame.

In 1934 the Great Depression was in full bloom and the only help poor people had were their family and the church. The Scarlato family moved to 177 Classon Avenue, which was a three family apartment house owned by Carmela's father, Salvatore — "Ta Ta". In the first floor apartment lived Domenick's grandfather, with his third wife, Maria, and two children, Rafael and Frances. On the second floor were his Aunt Angie and Uncle Frank, who acted like Domenick's parents as they had no children of their own. The new arrivals lived on the third floor in a "Coal Water" four-room apartment. The only heat they had in the winter was a big black coal stove in the kitchen. There was no bathroom, but they had a toilet the size of a telephone booth.

This was an era where Time stood still. It was a society in which progress was stagnant. This area of Brooklyn still had horse-drawn wagons delivering ice to residents' ice boxes. Push carts filled with fruits and vegetables were stretched along the main thoroughfare, Myrtle Avenue. This avenue had all types of stores, trolley cars, and an elevated train constantly driving by. It was always busy with shoppers. Domenick was a second generation Italian-American raised only one block from Myrtle Avenue. Only four blocks away were the East River docks, an area surrounded by factories, garages, and junk yards. It was a Brooklyn slum area, which in today's terms is called a ghetto — a misnomer. Domenick's mother always complained about the black soot from the four stack Power Plant — six blocks away — which formed daily on window sills and clothes line. The plant provided electricity to a large section of Brooklyn. At each end of their block were a paint factory and a rubber factory. In the middle of the block was a huge fifteen-truck garage. And, next door to the coal water apartment was horse and wagon stable.

Domenick spent many a day throwing rocks at the rats which came from the stable into the backyard to feast off vegetables planted by his grandfather. This was fun. Fortunately none of the huge rats came into the apartments. So the boy believed, anyway. Another pastime was petting and talking to the horses that poked their heads out through the open stable windows which faced his backyard.

On Domenick's block lived various ethnic and racial poor families, Italians, Irish, Polish, Jewish, and Colored (Black) families. In his class at P. S. 157 there were at least three or four Black children present. Everyone got along. But sometimes "gangs" from other neighborhoods came around looking for trouble. Once Domenick, seven years old, was playing in the Taffee Place playground, which was located around the corner from where he lived. He was wearing his favorite hat, an Aviator's Cap. Some Black kids from another neighborhood arrived, and an older boy approached Domenick and demanded his hat. He refused, so the older boy grabbed the cap and used it to hit Domenick in the face. Metal goggles on the cap stung like a hundred bees. Domenick went into a rage and attacked the other boy, pounding his head on the concrete sidewalk. If the park attendant did not stop the fight, the other boy might have ended up in the hospital. It was Domenick's first fight. It wouldn't be his last.

His neighborhood extended beyond his block, and all of Domenick's relatives lived within a ten-block radius from his apartment house. Grandfather Domenico "Nonni" Scarlato and grandmother, Christina "Nanni," lived around the corner on Myrtle Avenue and Taffee Place. Domenick always visited his grandparents at least once a week, even when he was in his late twenties. They were especially close.

From seven to thirteen years old, the boy played like all of the boys in these slums, ghettoes. Sandlot baseball, basketball, handball, and swimming in the East River. They built "club houses" in vacant lots, and went into "haunted houses" — vacant homes — to cut out lead pipes. They sold the lead pipes to Junk Yards.

In 1938, how does a kid get money for ice cream, candy, or a cigarette? He would cash in bottles for the deposits, or scavenge around to find something to sell to the junkman. In those days lead sold for five cents a pound. The times were the tail end of the Depression and money was very scarce. There were still bread lines, soup kitchens, and kids starving. A score of twenty pounds of lead earned a kid one dollar. A dollar went a long way. A pack of cigarettes cost thirteen cents, single cigarettes one penny, when available. An ice cream bar was five cents. One could go on and on, but a kid could be motivated to steal lead from old abandoned houses. A lot of kids believed that abandoned houses were *haunted*.

Another incident occurred when Domenick and the DeLeo brothers were cutting out lead from some condemned houses, which were scheduled to be torn down to make room for the first low income projects to be built in New York City. The projects would be called the Fort Greene Projects. Domenick, Frankie, and Rico worked many a night, avoiding the night watchmen, to cut out the lead pipes. After five nights they had accumulated over a hundred pounds of lead. This was to be their biggest caper. Since they could not carry this much lead, they concluded that they needed a wagon to haul it to the junkyard. One night they came and loaded up a wagon with the hard-earned bounty. Since there were night watchmen, the boys acted like commandos and worked right under their noses. As the boys pulled the heavy laden wagon along Flushing Avenue they were stopped by a police patrol car. Two cops got out and forced the boys against a wall. They were very rough and asked the boys where they got the lead. The boys said they found it along the street. The cops slapped them around, but the boys stuck to their story. The cops took the boys names and said that they were giving the kids a break. They said they didn't want to see their faces again. With that, the cops put the wagon and the lead piping into the patrol car and drove off. The three boys just looked at each other, shrugged their shoulders, and went home. Tomorrow was another day.

The kids played in the streets with such games as, "Kicking the Can," "Johnny on the pony," and "Tag on the Roof-No Touching the Ground." Domenick, at 10 years old, fell—or was pushed—off a two storey roof. The kids started yelling for him to get up. His reply was he felt like his arm was into the ground. An older cousin, Dolly, raced to his aid. When she picked him up into her arms, his left arm dangled and he screamed and passed out. He woke up sitting in a chair in Mr. Block's drug store. All the people were staring in through the large drug store window. It seemed like an eternity for the ambulance to arrive. Domenick was wearing a sweat shirt which had a "G-man's" badge and gun belt stenciled on the shirt. When the paramedic cut the sleeve off his sweat shirt, the boy began to cry. He cried not for the great pain in his arm and shoulder, but because his sweat shirt was ruined. The supposed doctor at Beth Moses Hospital, with two attendants, put Domenick under a phlorescope and said, "Here's the break in the left arm, and the shoulder is dislocated." With no anesthesia, all three men proceeded to pull hard on Domenick's left arm. His screams were so loud that his mother heard them on the next floor. He passed out. After he was revived he found himself with his left arm against his chest and all taped up like a mummy. He was told to get off the table and rejoin his mother. When Domenick got off the table he was very wobbly and his mother had to help him leave the hospital.

It was late at night. There were no cabs or traffic. These were the Depression years. No one had telephones, and there were few cars. With his mother's help, Domenick walked three long blocks to Myrtle Avenue. They waited a long time for the trolley to take them home.

After two weeks, his arm was still swollen and ached tremendously. His mother took him to their family doctor. Who removed—painfully to Domenick—all of the excess tape around the boy's body. The doctor stated that the arm had started to develop an infection of gangrene. If Domenick did not get to a hospital quickly for an operation, he would lose his arm or die. There were no antibiotics in those days. The doctor personally drove the boy and his mother to Cumberland Street Hospital. There a doctor had to re-break Domenick's arm and perform a lengthy operation. It took almost three years of therapy and exercises to regain full use of the arm. All this trouble because an incompetent doctor and staff had improperly set the break, and put on too much tape which cut off the blood circulation. Domenick was lucky to have survived this horrendous ordeal.

The exercises, weight training, and swimming at the Y.M.C.A. made his left arm more powerful than his right arm. It also caused Domenick to develop a very fit and strong body.

Even though Domenick's parents were born in America, they were very traditional in their ways and extremely strict in their methods of disciplining their children. Though European in many ways, they spoke only English at home. It should be noted that Damiano had two years of high school, while Carmela left school after the 6th Grade. The parents were patriotic Americans, and their patriotism was instilled into the children. Domenick, first born, was the couple's first experience in raising children. And, the oldest son had to be a role model for his brother, five years younger, and his sister, ten years younger. He had to help take care of them, watch over them, plus be responsible for their actions. This pressure and environment caused Domenick to develop some hostility toward his parents — and the outside world. Although he excelled in P. S. 157 elementary school, Domenick became a delinquent in high school and a terror on the streets.

The first major "rumble," one of many, occurred when Domenick took his younger brother, Salvatore, to The Summer Garden. The park had various children's rides, such as a large snake slide, a self-propelled merry-go-round, swings, and others. It was situated two city blocks away from Domenick's home, and half a block away from the 88th Precinct Police Station. Domenick, 12, made sure that Salvatore, 7, did not get hurt on the rides. They both had a good time that day. They finally left for home in good spirits. While walking, three boys came out from an apartment house and approach the two brothers. The older and much larger boy told Domenick that "Guineas" from below Myrtle Avenue were not welcome at The Summer Garden. It was typical then that some Irish did not like Italians. Domenick ignored the comment and kept walking, with Salvatore behind. All of a sudden he heard his younger brother scream. When he turned around, he saw Salvatore on the ground, and one of the other boys near him with a stick. Domenick went into a rage, and rushed that boy, knocking him out with a hard right cross. He then turned to the larger boy and with a flurry of punches dropped him as well. The third boy took off running. When Domenick couldn't catch him, he stopped at an Ice Wagon and grabbed the ice pick off the back of the wagon. He threw the ice pick, which imbedded into the boy's leg. With that done, he picked up his younger brother and they both ran home. That was the last time they went to The Summer Garden.

TWO - The Adventurer

Hollywood has always influenced the public in many ways. This is especially true for the younger generation.

Way back, the Cowboy was always the icon in Cinema. In silent movies, William S. Hart was the role model for kids who wanted to be cowboys. This was true in Domenick's father's time, 1906 to 1928, and so on. Characters such as Tim Holt, Buck Jones, the Lone Ranger, Gene Autry, etc, were admired by everyone. Most kids got over wanting to be cowboys when they grew older. But some kids who were able to be exposed to horses, became quasi-cowboys.

The would-be cowboy who became known as the "Brooklyn Cowboy" was a kid named Domenick Scarlato. He was raised in a slum area of Brooklyn that had various ethnic and racial groups, who got along. And, next to his house, was a Horse and Wagon Stable. He used to give sugar, pet, and talk to the horses who stuck their heads out the open windows. At the age of ten, he began to help Pete, the owner of the stable, clean stalls, etc. He loved to be near horses. By the time he was thirteen, Domenick used to hitch onto the back of trolley car and travel to Prospect Park. At the end of the park, at Ocean Parkway, was a riding academy. Domenick worked there part-time, for free, so he could ride on a horse. He escorted people who rented the riding horses and took rides through Prospect Park. The huge park had a very large lake,, a zoo, and bridle path. Soon, Domenick could ride any horse except a bucking bronco. He even took Salvatore and taught him to ride through Prospect Park.

At 13, Domenick was tall, husky, and strong from lifting weights and exercising to recuperate his arm. He was often treated like an adult. At local movie houses he had to pay adult prices because they did not believe his actual age. And, he started to hang out with older boys, who belonged to street gangs. Here Domenick excelled in fighting, so he moved up the ladder in the pecking order of the gang. For this, he thanked his parents for his tough upbringing. Domenick could take anything anyone had to dish out and give it back in spades. Wherever he went, in or out of his neighborhood, his reputation preceded him.

13 YEARS OLD

Although he was tough and could fight the big guys, Domenick had not yet matured mentally. He had a lot to learn about staying out of trouble. He was too easily influenced by older boys. One such boy was James Fazio. One night, Fazio convinced Domenick and two other boys to join him on a "night raid." Assuming an exciting adventure, the three boys followed Fazio to a closed candy store. Fazio threw a large rock through the door-window, and told the boys to cover the opening when he went inside. The three boys stood in front of the opening—and in a moment began to sing songs. Suddenly four police cars converged. The cops began yelling at them and beating them about their bodies with night sticks. They were taken to the station house, where the detectives began scaring the daylights out of them. The next day they were transported to the Children's Shelter at Schemerhorn Street, Boro Hall, Brooklyn. James Fazio, who was over sixteen years old, was taken to the Raymond Street Jail—known as "The Tombs." The week stay at the Shelter was a horror. Inside were approximately sixty to seventy "kids" ranging in age ten to fifteen years old. Everyone ate small amounts of beans or stews, and slept in large dormitories. The guards were cruel and strict. There were at least twenty Colored kids in the Shelter, and some would "gang-up" on a White kid. Domenick had this experience with four Black kids while in the toilet. The bigger and older Black boy intimidated him and punched him in the jaw. Reacting as he usually did, Domenick knocked that boy down and pushed his way passed the other three. No one there bothered him again. In fact, he was then called "Crazy Nick."

Domenick was placed on probation and sent home, as the judge saw that he had been used as a dupe. James Fazio was sent to "reform school," a much tougher sentence for juveniles. Later, Fazio would spend more time in prisons than out of them. No need to go into detail as to what happened when Domenick got home — but it was not a welcoming party. A new strict surveillance by his parents, following every move he made, caused him to drift further and further away from his own neighborhood.

As rough as Domenick was, he did have a good heart, a feel for fair play, plus a good Christian background. One day he and his close friend, Tony "Blonde" Mastriano, were traveling on the Myrtle Avenue "EL," which has outdoor trains above the street. They got off at Franklin Avenue Station and saw a woman, who had been shopping for Christmas, fall off the platform and onto the tracks. A fast-moving train was coming and the chances of stopping it were nil. Domenick jumped down onto the tracks and began trying to lift the very heavy woman up onto the platform. Tony also jumped down to help his friend. Together they managed to get the woman up to safety. The boys climbed up just in the nick of time as the train roared into the station.

Instead of thanking the boys for saving her life, the woman only worried about her packages. "Who is going to get my packages?" she kept saying. As the people on the platform comforted the woman, the boys were ignored.

Domenick said to Tony, "Blonde, that's okay. People are funny that way." And the two friends walked away.

At this juncture of time, Chelsea Vocational High School for Domenick was becoming troublesome and a waste of time. There were too many Black and White confrontations. He also felt that his desire to learn was being stifled and his numerous talents wasted, even though he was always energetic and eager to learn. He had done excellent work at P.S. 157 Elementary. Chelsea Vocational was a dumping ground for undesirables.

He had been advised to go there by a teacher who did not know anything about the school. She had read that it had an aviator and aviation mechanic program. Domenick loved airplanes.

Domenick loved the arts. He was always drawing. He made large posters for the school to promote War Bond drives for the war effort. He and Angelo Gargano painted an 8ft. x 30ft. wall mural, a scene depicting mountains, forests, lakes, and rivers, with a realistic Indian village. The mural was painted on a wall in the auditorium and stayed there for over twenty years. When Domenick asked a teacher about art schools, he was told that fine artists starved, and, commercial artists were usually a father and son deal. He was advised to be an aviation mechanic. Actually, this sounded exciting, especially with the War and the need for pilots and mechanics.

So a thirteen year old "graduate' traveled each day to Chelsea Vocational High School, from Brooklyn to Manhattan by subway, only to find a façade of an aviation program. Domenick attended school faithfully for one year. But he began playing hooky and going to Times Square to sneak into movies with his friend, Artie "Blackie" Sporenza.

Eventually, Domenick started to go downtown and hang out with the "Navy Street Boys." That gang hung out at a pool room which catered to petty crooks and mobsters who were connected. He was only fifteen years old, but by now had the good sense to not work for any of these gangsters. He was offered many times to go on jobs, such as a fur heist or a high-jacking a ship's cargo. Domenick always graciously refused, and he also kept his mouth shut. He just wanted the excitement of belonging to the Navy Street Boys and to be recognized as a tough, loyal, and reliable guy.

The "Boys" traveled in many a fashion, hitching rides on the back of trolley cars, trucks, or whatever could take them somewhere for free. No one believed in paying for anything. They sneaked in to every theater in downtown Brooklyn, and in every theater in Times Square. To pay to go to a show was a sin.

There were many gangs in Brooklyn, Manhattan, and Bronx. Rivalry was rampid. Whenever you went somewhere you never knew who you would fight. One such incident occurred at the Fox Theater, one of downtown Brooklyn's largest, which had Amateur Night on Mondays. Singers, dancers, and other performers came from all over New York City. Also drawn to the Fox were gangs such as The Red Hook Boys, Red Skin Rumbles, Blue Birds, Greenpoint Maulers, and so on. They took command of both balconies. It was inevitable that a fight would break out between two or more gangs. This got so bad that the Fox eventually had to have Special Police patrol the aisles. One Monday night during a fight, one policeman was thrown off the balcony. Fox discontinued Monday Amateur Night. The newspapers never printed stories about gang wars because World War II dominated the news.

In school one day, Domenick had a confrontation — one of many — with a Black boy, older and bigger. At fifteen, Domenick was 5'10" tall and weighed 160 pounds. He was very strong. Playing sports, plus his rough lifestyle, made him quite an adversary to challenge. He had trouble with Blacks before but always managed to get out of it. On this day the two boys met in the schoolyard and began to fight. Domenick was getting the best of his bigger challenger. Suddenly six or seven Blacks surrounded Domenick and started beating on him. He managed to break through and made a run for it. Badly bruised and beaten, he went to the pool room where the Navy Street Boys hung out. When the gang saw and heard what had been done, they stated that they would be at the school yard the next day at 3:00 P.M. They told Domenick to pick another fight with the same Black boy. Ten guys would be lying in wait. They would make sure it was a fair fight. If it wasn't, they would take care of the [blank] Black bastards. Sure enough, Domenick encountered the Black boy again in the schoolyard. Again he was beating the other boy, and again he was surrounded by the same Black group. With that ten Navy Street Boys came out with bats and chains. It was a bloody mess. Someone called the police. All of Domenick's friends got away. He did not.

He had knocked out the boy who had started the first fight. He also knocked out another Black boy. Then someone hit him in the back of his head. He fell to his knees, and two policemen grabbed his arms. Since fighting in or on school grounds was not a real crime, the policemen took him to the principal's office. They threw him into a small chair and told the principal, "He's your problem. Take care of it."

The principal, Mr. McQue, began blaming Domenick for all of the trouble. Being so dazed, the young man could barely make out what the principal was saying. Finally his head began to clear and he could hear Principal McQue berating him.

Domenick said, "Where were you when there were problems all throughout the year? Where were you when I was ganged up on and beaten yesterday? Where were you when they ganged up on me again today? A bunch of guys saved me today from being sent to a hospital, or killed by those Blacks. You call my guys hoods? They should be congratulated for saving my life!."

The principal again called Domenick a trouble maker. He also called him a "Guinea from Brooklyn." With that, Domenick hit the principal so hard he knocked him out. Needless to say, Domenick was expelled from Chelsea Vocational High School.

In July, Domenick made a long trip to New Jersey to visit his Aunt Matilda, Uncle Tom, and his cousins — Frank and Tommy Lanzana. He started off in a trolley car, then took the subway all the way to 179th Street, and the George Washington Bridge. From there he rode a bus to Norwood, New Jersey. Domenick had an unusual value of respect. He believed faithfully in visiting his aunt and relatives wherever they were.

He had done this long trip before, which was very unusual for a fifteen year old boy. Most of Grandma "Nanni" Scarlato's family had settled in Norwood. Everyone there knew Domenick as "The Kid from Brooklyn," who when he spent time at his Aunt Matilda's house he was as wild as they come. To all of the Norwood kids, Domenick was a "Big G," someone from New York City who was tough, hip, sharp, and cool.

To illustrate a story which showed how wild Domenick was: All the kids in Norwood looked up to him as they figured he was from Brooklyn, so he must know all the angles. In late evenings an ice cream truck used to come into the small town of Norwood. He told each kid to keep the ice cream man busy, because when he opens the rear door to get the ice cream bars a light bulb on the dashboard lights up. While the man is at the rear of the truck, Domenick will slip in the front door and turn off the bulb. This way when the truck goes away he could hitch on the back tailgate. He could then open the door and throw out all of the ice cream bars for the kids to pick up. The plan sounded good, except the truck took off to fast and as Domenick hopped on the tailgate he could not reach far enough to open the door. The truck was traveling so fast that he figured he had better get off. He figured God knows where he would end up as it was pitch black outside. He tried to run with the truck as to get the momentum of speed. This he had done many times with trolley cars and city trucks but this time it did not work. He fell tumbling head over heals on the asphalt road.

The only thing Domenick remembered was that he told the kids not to say anything to anybody. He then blacked out mentally, even though he was conscious and spoke normally to everyone. His memory came back to him when he felt an ice pack on his head and realized that his grandmother from Brooklyn was holding the ice pack.

"Nanni, when did you get here?" he asked.

"I've been here for two days, don't you remember? You hugged and kissed me."

No one believed that he could not remember. Domenick had lost two days, and he never recovered them.

This bad experience of course did not stop him from occasionally visiting his aunt in New Jersey. He loved Aunt Matilda very much, and he liked to travel like a gypsy.

All the kids admired Domenick. There was one girl, named Margaret, who had a crush on him. She followed him wherever he went. He liked Margaret, but considered her as a sister. One day she told him to listen to a song. "…because it will tell you how I feel about you. That song, sung by Vaughn Monroe, was "There I said it again." Domenick is now in his autumn years and when he hears this song he still remembers Margaret. It is a happy song of love, yet it makes him very blue. He didn't realize then how dear she was to him.

In the town of Norwood there lived a rich family named the Bienquista. Mr. John Bienquista owned a large heavy-equipment contracting company. His son was called "Junior" by everyone. Junior liked horses. On the family's five acre estate, there was a barn with a corral, and two horses, which Junior and his sister rode often. When junior went riding he always wore the proper riding attire. The entire Bienquista family was always very proper.

When Domenick was in town it was said that all of the kids flocked around him. He was The Brooklyn Kid from "the Big City," and he always led them on some exciting adventure. These adventures were sometimes good, sometimes bad, but always exciting. Somehow Junior did not take to Domenick very well. Whenever Domenick spoke, Junior would always challenge his statement or story. As an example, there was a time when Domenick said he could ride any horse except a bronco.

"How can a Brooklyn kid be a cowboy?" Junior demanded to know. "Prove it. Let us see you ride a horse."

"Get me a horse. I'll prove it."

Junior smiled and said, "Come to my house. I have horses." The Bienquista family then had five horses.

So Domenick, Margaret, and four other kids went to Junior's estate home.

Junior was a shrewd kid. At the barn, he saddled a horse which had a bad habit of brushing riders along the corral fence. Domenick mounted the horse and began to ride around the corral. On the first pass the horse brushed him against the fence, bruising his right leg. Domenick realized the horse's trickery and lifted up his right leg and placed it over the horn of the saddle. He then made three circles without incident. He told one of the other kids to open the corral gate. Quickly Domenick goaded the horse out and rode around the meadow. After a time, he rode the horse back into the corral.

"Thanks for the ride, Junior. I can break that horse's bad habit of brushing the fence if you want me to."

Junior did not respond.

All of the kids cheered and called Domenick "The Brooklyn Cowboy."

On one July trip to New Jersey he met a beautiful blonde fourteen year old girl, named Vickie Nigro, who the Jersey kids said was from Brooklyn. Domenick did not believe them. When they told him that she lived in the same building, as his Uncle Sal and Aunt Angie Scarlato, on Bedford Avenue, he said they were trying to pull a fast one. He would not believe them. He went back to Brooklyn not believing that Vickie Nigro could be living in the same building as his Uncle Sal. He had visited his uncle many times in the past and never saw such a girl as Vickie.

Domenick usually went to the YMCA at least three times each week to workout. On his next trip, he made a point of stopping by Uncle Sal's apartment. As he approached the building, there was Vickie sitting on the stoop, smiling like a Cheshire Cat.

"What are you doing here?"

"My father owns this building, and this is where I live, silly."

Domenick was stunned.

She continued. "I've been sitting on this stoop every evening, just to see if you would pass by."

"How did you know I would?"

"The Norwood kids told me that you went to the "Y" and that you took Bedford when you walked home. So, here I am"

"Okay…"

"You know, if you felt something for me, you could have looked me up."

"Well, I just did."

He began seeing Vickie each time he went to the Y. They would sit on the stoop and talk, talk, and talk.

One evening when Domenick came to see Vickie, her mother, Josephine, was sitting on the stoop in the place where Vickie would normally sit. She spoke to him in a very nice calm gentle voice. She said that she knew everyone in his family. In fact she went to school with his uncles. That their people were *piazanos* from the same town in Italy, and that she did not want any trouble with his family. She said Vickie and he were too young to be seeing each other so much. She said that if he really loved her daughter he will come back when he is of age. As hard as it was he respected her wishes and said someday he will return.

While Domenick worked out at the Y, some men in the know advised him that he should take up regular boxing. He had a lot of potential, they said. So he began to train. But he still lifted weights fervently. He also loved to swim, which he learned to do in the East River. Consequently he developed even more strength and power, which would later help him in the U. S. Navy. Domenick boxed amateur boxing, PAL (Police Athletic League), CYO (Catholic Youth Organization), and the Ridgewood Grove. He won many bouts. Ettore Penn, who fought Tommy Morelli, said that Domenick "...could take punishment, can give it, has heart, and has a deadly knockout punch." Ettore said that he had a good future in boxing and that he should go professional.

However, Domenick's career in boxing was cut short because of "run-in with law." One night one of the fellows, named Funzi, told Domenick and three other Navy Street Boys that he had his brother's truck and asked them if they wanted to take a ride to Coney Island. Everyone was elated and they climbed into the truck. As they proceeded along Ocean Parkway, Funzi ran a red light. A police car pulled them over. The truck turned out to be stolen. Even though the four boys told the police that they were innocent passengers—and Funzi verified this—the police took them in. Domenick had just turned sixteen, so he and the others were taken to the Raymond Street Jail, know as The Tombs. This experience shook up Domenick as he was placed in a cell like "The Big House," a penitentiary.

His trial took very little time as the case was dismissed. What helped him were the facts that he was only a passenger, and he had served as an Air Raid Messenger. In case of an air raid, and power was knocked out, he would take messages from one police precinct to others. He also became a certified Air Raid Warden. Grand larceny charges were dropped, but the judge placed Domenick into a Wayward Minor Program—"Hanging around with known criminals." He was now on probation.

Although Domenick hung out with the Navy Street crowd, he did work part-time at many jobs after school and during the summer. To note, all the money he made working he brought home to his mother and she gave him a small allowance. To Domenick he was satisfied because he felt he was helping the family.

In the years 1939 to 1943, Domenick found many ways to make money. Illicit jobs such as taking empty bottles for their deposit, scavenging lead and copper from abandoned houses, and making slugs to use on the subway or candy machines was the petty way to find some independence. There were some jobs which could be considered legitimate but they were really exploitation. At age eleven he had worked in a grocery store. At twelve he worked on a horse and wagon delivering ice. He loaded beer trucks when he was thirteen. At fourteen he worked part-time nights in a bread factory. The pay was always menial, but good enough to bring home to his mother. She kept most of it but he did get a small allowance, which was more than he would have if he never worked.

THREE - The Docks

Domenick had a good friend named Artie Speranza, whose nickname was "Blackie". Blackie was seventeen, and so he was a mentor to him, who learned how to sneak into every theater in downtown Brooklyn and uptown Manhattan. He could have been a great "second story' man, but he was honest in his own way.

One day Blackie asked Domenick if he would be interested in working on the docks with him.

"I hear you have to 'shape up' to work on the waterfront," said the younger Domenick.

"That's right. But I have connections."

He told Domenick that he had an uncle who was Dock Foreman at the Bush Terminal in South Brooklyn. Now Domenick knew that longshoremen got union wage, which meant good money. He did not hesitate.

"Okay. When do we start?"

"Meet me at six o'clock tomorrow morning. We have to be at the docks to shape-up at seven."

To do this, Domenick had to play hooky from school. They both arrived at the docks at Seven O'clock sharp and lined up to be picked for work. Domenick was young, but he fitted in well with the men because he was muscular and stronger than the average man.

Blackie's uncle was a big burly man, who was not only Dock Foreman but also a Longshoremen's Union representative. He wore an old fedora hat with five matches in the hat band. Blackie said that the five matches represented the five dollar "kick-back" to his uncle if he picked you out of the line-up. His uncle walked up and down the line choosing men to work that day. Blackie and Domenick were selected, and the men not selected had to come back and try another day. To Domenick this seemed so unfair. He felt sorry for the men turned away.

He said to Blackie, "What about the men who have a family to support?"

Blackie answered, "Life is tough and you have to have connections."

Domenick was seeing the real world and he did not like it very much.

While working unloading freighters, Domenick observed that every now and then a box would be deliberately dropped by the crane operator. The contents would spill out. Those contents disappeared quickly. He also noted that late in the day an unmarked truck would back up to have many of the boxes loaded onto it. The truck then sped off. When Domenick brought this to Blackie's attention, his friend warned him to keep his mouth shut.

"You must be like the three monkeys — see no evil, hear no evil, speak no evil."

Domenick got the message loud and clear.

He gave his mother half of what he earned. He didn't tell her that he was working on the waterfront during the day, but instead said he was working at night in one of the machine shops making war products. In those days you were not paid by checks. They paid you in cash, in an envelope. His mother and father believed him. This façade enabled him to stay out late every night. With money in his pocket and free to roam, he was able to hangout with his friends from the Navy Street pool room.

This arrangement lasted for about three months before a terrible occurrence caused Domenick to consider quitting his job. Well liked by his fellow workers, he was also trusted. Word got around that one longshoreman, who was not well liked, did something against the group. Everyone was told to stay clear of this individual. Domenick heeded the warning. One morning this individual was working in the hole of a ship, loading cargo into a large net to be hauled up by the boom. Then it happened. The boom let loose and the entire cargo in the net crashed down on the man, killing him instantly. Domenick witnessed this killing. Although upset inside himself, he kept his cool.

Two weeks later, he told Blackie that he appreciated everything his friend did for him, but that the job was putting a strain on the family. He hated to give up a good thing but he couldn't afford trouble with his mother and father. Blackie understood, and so did his uncle.

"You're a good worker, kid. I like you. If you ever want to come back, you'll be welcome."

FOUR - First Love

During World War II, the shortage of men for the workforce was in dire straits. Even though women were taking the place of men in war plants, the civilian markets were lacking.

During this time, some of Domenick's friends called him "Nicky." The DeLeo brothers, good friends, were working in a leather tanning place, a small plant in lower Manhattan near Park Row. The owner of this tanning business, a heavy moustached, cigar-smoking man named Silverstein, needed help. Frank and Ricco DeLeo advised Nicky. Since high school was ending for the summer, Nicky said he would take the job. It paid ten dollars for a forty hour week. He would have to take the Myrtle Avenue trolley downtown to the Brooklyn Bridge and then walk across the bridge.

The job was rough. He had to unload bales of raw leather, weighing up to 400 pounds, from trucks using bailing hooks. Handtrucks were used to take them inside. Tanning involved large vats of chemicals to pickle and process the raw leather. Wet sheets were stretched and stapled onto large boards to dry. Working conditions were hot, dirty, and stinking. Only fifteen, Nicky was mature, as well as strong from weight-lifting, running the track, handball, and swimming at the YMCA.

Nicky was very family oriented, with traditions and obedience to his family. His $10.00 weekly, in a brown envelope, went to his mother, unopened. For this, he received a $2.00 allowance, which covered carfare, and small pleasures. Silverstein liked the way Nicky worked. In fact, each time a DeLeo brother was fired, for one reason or another, the owner gave Domenick a $1.00 raise. Suddenly he was making $12.00 a week.

Nicky always brought his lunch from home. Usually a large Italian bread "hero" and Nicky would sit on the steps of the building to eat. Because of the heat inside, and the July heat outside, he was usually shirtless. The outdoor breeze felt good on his bare chest. In an area of small industry and small business, the street was always full of people walking by. Nicky loved to "people watch," especially the girls. There was one particular girl who really caught his eye with her beauty. He blue eyes, long black hair, and gorgeous body caused him to whistle when she passed. She just walked on. On the third day she passed, Nicky got up enough nerve to talk to her. She responded by asking why he took so long to speak. They had a nice conversation. Her name was Marie, and she was from the Bronx. Nicky took her telephone number, which was to a candy store. It is to be noted that in 1943 very few people had telephones in their homes. The candy store was owned by the father of Marie's good friend, Margaret. Eventually Nicky made a date with Marie.

It was a very long ride to the Bronx. It took one and a half hours and two subway changes to reach Marie's home. It was funny how girls on their first date had to have their girl friend come along—on a double date. So it was with Marie. Nicky convinced his close friend, Tony "Blonde," to come along. It is to be noted that Nicky was 15, Tony, 16. Marie was 19 years old, and her friend, Margaret, was 20 years old. The girls did not know the boys' ages.

This first date, on a Saturday, was to the Bronx Zoo. By the time the two couples arrived at the zoo, they were compatible. Both girls seemed to enjoy the boys' company. When viewing the Bronx Zoo, it was very different than regular zoos. At a regular zoo all of the animals are in cages, and there is no forest or foliage. At the Bronx Zoo, one sees green grass and thick trees. With all of the greenery, a clear sky, and cool breeze, this day was beautiful. After visiting various fenced-in animals, the foursome strolled towards a large hill. On top of this hill, they suddenly saw two large lions. The lions stared at them. Nicky and Tony froze for a moment, and they then began yelling at the top of their lungs. "The lions are loose!" While repeating this warning, they grabbed the girls and ran for cover. Everyone at the zoo was at first shocked, but they began to laugh. The girls were laughing too. When the boys calmed down, the girls told them that there was a water-filled moat around the hill. The lions could not reach them. Nicky and Tony felt like fools. But the girls stated that they loved the fact that the two boys had bravely tried to save them.

Finally the couple moved closer to the island-hill in order to get a closer look at the lions. It was a delightful afternoon.

That evening, they had pizza for dinner and went to Crotona Park. Nicky pulled his buddy aside.

"Tony, me and Marie are gonna sit on another bench, so we can talk, you know?"

Tony was naïve—and worried. "No, Nicky. I don't know how to talk to a girl alone. What am I gonna do?"

"Tony, just look at me and do whatever I do."

So when they got to the park and the couples sat on different benches, Tony watched every move Nicky made. It was to say a comical scene as Nicky got close to Marie, Tony got close to Margaret, and so on and so on. When Nicky and Marie got up and walked away, Tony panicked and started yelling for his buddy.

Nicky and Marie quickly came running back. "What is wrong? Why are you yelling? Nicky asked Tony.

Tony blushed and was speechless. Nicky and Marie sat down with their friends, and the night ended with a good laugh.

After dating Marie for three months, he told her is real name, being Domenick—and that he was fifteen years old. She said it did not matter as she loved him very much.

"But, Nicky—Domenick—please don't tell my two sisters."

As time passed their age differences didn't matter. They drew close to each other like two peas in a pod. Marie told Domenick that when they were together she felt they were as one.

A very funny, then again not so funny, incident occurred. He contracted two ringworms on the upper part of his thigh. He probably got them from swimming in the Red Hook Pool. They looked so bad and itched violently. Tony told Nicky that he had read that to soak the ringworms with bleach would kill them and soothe the itch. Domenick, being ignorant to medicine and treatments, believed his friend. He stripped off his pants and underwear, and with Tony directing, put bleach on the infected areas. In a few minutes his thighs were on fire. Domenick quickly tried to rinse his thighs with water but that only seemed to make it worse. The burning made him go crazy. He yelled at the top of his lungs and went after Tony. Tony ran out of the apartment building as fast as he could. Domenick began to punch a metal cabinet which held some dishes. The cabinet was dented, but amazingly none of the dishes broke. His mother, who was downstairs in her sister Angie's apartment, came running up the stairs. Hearing his mother coming, Domenick locked the door. She pleaded for him to let her in. Finally he got control of himself and opened the door. When he told her what had happened, his mother prepared a paste which she applied to the ringworms. The paste did soothe his thighs. Domenick could not have loved his mother any more than that day.

The infected skin literally peeled off. The paste did its job. But Domenick could hardly walk. He had to walk with his legs apart.

Now, as it so happened on this ill-fated weekend, Domenick had a date with Marie. He asked Tony to call her and explain why he could not make this date. It must be remembered that in the Depression poor people did not have telephones. So Tony called Marie from a garage across the street from the apartment buildings. Instead of trying to explain exactly what happened, Tony kept it short. He told her that Domenick had broken his leg, and that he would call her when he was well. Tony never told Domenick this minor detail.

The next weekend, he was feeling a little better, but he had to wear a padded jockstrap in order to walk sort of normally. It was the only way he could keep the irritated areas from rubbing together.

Tony said, "You know, all week we have stayed home. Maybe we should go to Coney Island, just to look around."

"That's a good idea. The ride isn't too far, and I can walk slowly when we get there."

When Domenick and Tony arrived at Coney Island it was a great feeling for both of them. Lights, music, the noise of the rides and the crowd, were exhilarating. They walked through Luna Park—which later burned down—among the many side shows. Each show had its own booth and a stage showing freaks like The Bearded lady, Alligator Boy, Three headed Cow, or Dancing Arabian girls. Standing in front of the booth for The Sword Swallowing Man, Domenick and Tony heard a female voice behind them.

"You recovered from your broken leg quickly, I see."

Domenick turned around slowly and was shocked to see Marie and Margaret standing there. He could not believe his eyes. What a coincidence that his girl had come all the way from the Bronx to visit Coney Island for her first time, and she met him among thousands of people. It was and is unbelievable. Domenick was dumbfounded, embarrassed, and speechless.

It finally occurred to him to ask, "What broken leg?"

"Tony said that you broke your leg, and that was why you couldn't make our date."

Domenick stared at Tony, who was embarrassed.

It took a lot of explaining, by Tony and Domenick, to get the true story told. Marie forgave him for all of that, but she was still angry that he had not called her to say that he was feeling better. Domenick pleaded guilty and begged for her forgiveness. She finally mellowed, and the foursome, again, enjoyed Coney Island together.

Even though Marie completely forgave him and held no grudge, Domenick felt that he must do something for her. It can't be remembered how he found out the following information, but he learned that a very special, premier showing of Frank Sinatra's first movie, *Higher and Higher*, would be shown at the Spooner Theater on new Year's Eve. The opulent Spooner Theater was located on Simpson Boulevard, off Westchester Avenue, in the Bronx. To view this movie a person had to have reserved tickets for New Year's Eve. Domenick knew that Marie loved Frank Sinatra, so used his powerful connections to get tickets to this sold-out show. On New Year's Eve, Domenick "dressed up" in a suit and a tie, an overcoat, and a fedora hat. He felt so grown up. When he met Marie, she was dressed as a young beautiful lady. Her dress, accessories, and coat were outstanding. The two of them made a perfect couple.

"We're going to take in a movie," he told her.

Marie looked at him oddly. "Who goes to a movie on New Year's Eve?"

"We are going to a movie because we are different."

You are *different*."

"C'mon. You're going to like this."

When they arrived at the Spooner, and Marie saw the marquis displaying "Sinatra's First Picture – *Higher and Higher*, she was speechless. When she saw that reserved tickets were required, and could see that the theater was packed, she stared at him sadly.

"What's the matter with you? I have two reserved tickets."

She was so happy she hugged Domenick and cried.

They were seated on the first tier of the balconies. You could not have had better seats. They held hands throughout the movie. That New Year's Eve was a night never to be forgotten.

Unfortunately, love is not always smooth. A number of factors took their toll on this love affair. Late at night while traveling on subway trains, Domenick always seemed to attract "queers" who would proposition him. He always politely knocked them out and went on his way. The trip to Bronx took one and a half hours, and another one and a half back to Brooklyn. On some nights when he returned home late all hell broke loose at the Scarlato house. This put a strain on his relationship. Another strain was his newly found job his father's friend had given him at the Sanford Foundry Company.

Along with other men, this job was a multitask job of shoveling coal into giant blast furnaces, making sand molds, and pouring hot molten steel from large cauldrons into molds. Bomb casings were being made for the war effort. It was hard and tough work, and the men were constantly being burned.

Domenick used to come home from work and was not greeted with affection but with mistrust as to whether he went to work or not. His parents tried to restrict his going out at night. This led to many arguments. As stated previously, Domenick matured at a young age. He had always worked part-time after school and during summers. He had worked in a grocery store, a bakery factory, a machine shop, on an ice truck, and on the docks. Always seeking knowledge, he was willing to learn anything. Domenick read books, asked questions, and listened to the stories of his elders. He had been born with certain talents, such as art, music, and athletics. These were good traits which should have been nurtured. But because of strict upbringing, indifference, and narrowly focused guidance, Domenick went in the wrong direction by being driven out of his neighborhood. Today, when looking back, understanding what was needed, that was sorely lacking.

His run-ins with The Law, his oppressive parents, the strain on his love affair, and the horrible job at the foundry, caused Domenick to run away. America was fighting a World War. Even though he served as an Air Raid messenger and Air Raid warden, he thought to himself that he must do more for his country. With this in mind, he soon embarked on an adventure which would be filled with surprises. At the age of sixteen, Domenick decided to join the military.

FIVE - The Sailor

Along with a close friend named Tony "Stretch" Vallone, who was 6' 5" tall, Domenick went to the U. S. Recruiting Station and tried to enlist in the Marine Corps. At the recruiting station building were two offices, one for the Marine Corps and one for the Navy. As the two boys approached the Marines recruiting office, a Marine sergeant was closing the door. He said to them boys that he was going to lunch. "Come back later."

Domenick and Stretch were disappointed. But, lo and behold, the Navy office was open and the Chief Petty Officer on duty called out to them.

"Come on in, you guys. Let's talk."

He told them that the Marines didn't need them. "...See how the sergeant walked away from you? The United States Navy needs both of you."

The Chief was a smooth talker. Plus, Domenick had been brought up near the Brooklyn Navy Yard, and had encountered many Sailors in the area. His mother had an 18" x 30" picture of two-year-old Domenick in a Sailor suit. This picture hung in the family dining room for years. It only seemed natural that he should join the Navy.

He took the Navy enlistment form—stamped, "U. S. N.—and later forged his birth certificate and the signature on the form. While there, Domenick noticed other enlistment forms which were stamped, U. S. N. R.

"What's the difference with those forms?"

The Chief stated, with indifference, that those other forms were for the U. S. Navy Reserve, and the forms given to Domenick and Tony were "...for the Regular Navy."

"What's the difference?" Domenick asked again.

"The Reserves are in the War for the duration. If the war ends, they go home in six months. The Regular Navy men and women must stay and fulfill their four year commitment."

"Then isn't the Reserves better?"

"This war is going to last more than four years. Besides, the Navy treats "regulars" special, such as sending them to school, quicker rate increases, and better duty."

Domenick was street smart but naive to worldly matters, especially government issues and politics. The gullible sixteen-year-old accepted the Chief Petty Officer's words—a decision which would later come back to haunt him.

Another big mistake Domenick made was to enlist in October. Winters at the U. S. Navy's Great Lakes Boot Camp were usually between 30-degrees and 30-degrees below zero. Barracks were heated by pot belly stoves. Who was to know this? Certainly not Domenick Scarlato. Nor would the sly Chief at the recruiting office tell him. Cold times lay waiting.

When Domenick and Tony left New York City the weather was very mild. Both boys wore light windbreaker jackets. The train left Grand Central Station was a coach type and traveled like a "Cattle Car." It stopped at every town from NYC and Chicago. A normally nine-hour trip took thirty-six hours. The train was so packed with recruits that they had to literally sleep on others' shoulders. Tony sat next to a window, with his head and face pressed against the glass. Domenick slept leaning on Tony's shoulder, and another recruit, named Johnny Smith, slept against Domenick's shoulder. Passing through extremely cold country, the men huddled just to keep warm. This situation caused poor Tony to awake with his head and face half-frozen. He developed a severe headache.

The recruits arrived in Chicago at Eleven O'clock at night, and finally reached the Great Lakes Training Center at two in the morning. Approximately eighty recruits were hungry and cold. They were quickly given blankets and told to "Crap out" anywhere in the empty barracks. At 5:00 A.M. reveille sounded. The men were ushered into the mess hall for breakfast. Poor Tony complained about his headache, but no one paid him any attention. Domenick did his best to console his friend.

The food at the mess hall was something nobody had ever seen before. What was this creamy liquid with red pieces of meat stuck to it? It is called "S. O. S." the mess cook told them.

"It looks like vomit," Domenick said to Tony.

That morning all the recruits were told to strip naked and place all of their clothes in a box, which would be shipped to their homes. They were all given physicals and shots. It was a sight to see eighty naked men lined up to be examined by doctors, and get injections from sadistic Corpsmen who seemed to enjoy jabbing the needles into the recruits' arms. That afternoon, they were given their uniforms. Nobody seemed to get the correct size. Each was told that the sizes would "eventually work out."

Time for haircuts. Tony was a good-looking, very tall seventeen year old with dark brown eyes and hair. Domenick was a handsome 5' 10 ½" with light brown eyes and wavy light brown hair. Both boys wore their hair extra long—for that time—with the popular "D.A." duck's Ass cut. The navy's special service barbers were mostly southerners, called "hicks" by city people. These barbers loved to scalp city boys. It was painful for Domenick and Tony to emerge with their beautiful hair completely cut off. They were proclaimed "real patriots" or "bald eagles" by the other recruits who were merely given "crew cuts."

Tony still complained about his headaches, and finally he was separated from the others and sent to sick bay. One evening while the "boots" were relaxing in the barracks and writing letters, a Sailor appeared in dress blues. It was a rule that anyone in boot camp who did not have leggings could make a boot stand at attention, be saluted, and be called "sir." Upon seeing this Sailor appear in the barracks hall, the door watch sentry yelled, "Attention on deck!." Everyone jumped up and stood at attention. This Sailor approached each Boot and questioned him. Each Boot answered with a loud, "Yes Sir!." Finally Domenick saw this Sailor and realized that he was none other than Tony "Stretch" Vallone.

Domenick yelled, "The hell! This guy is no Sailor! While we dragged our butts for three weeks, this guy was in sick bay *goldbricking*!"

"I'm getting a medical discharge, on account of a punctured eardrum caused by an infection, caused by freezing one side of my head on that train. I'm going home in the morning."

"Bull! You can't leave me alone now! We were supposed to stick together, remember?"

"I don't have no choice." Tony got tears in his eyes.

The two buddies talked at length, and then Tony had to leave. Now Domenick was surely alone.

It is to be noted that Tony was later drafted into the Army.

Boot camp training was rough and tough, as the powers-to-be believed that a recruit must be broken down and then built back up again in order to fit the navy's discipline. They would drill you, embarrass you, harass you, and finally work you as hard as you could go. They trained you to be a team. They believed that alone you could make a mole hill, but together a team could make a mountain. To illustrate some examples: When snow on the "grinders," where the men would Drill or do PT exercises, was chest high the D. I. chief would have the Company of 160 boots form a column twenty men across and eight men deep. The entire column acted as a snow plow. Once the Chief ordered a squad of men to board a deuce-and-a-half truck, and they proceeded to the Great Lake—which was frozen over. The squad boarded a whale boat, and the Chief ordered the men to begin rowing, and he stressed teamwork.

The men said to the Chief that the lake was frozen, and so were the oars. How were they supposed to row, they asked.

"Simulate, my lads. Simulate!"

So simulate they did.

There were indoor classes and outdoor classes. Many were designed to teach the boots how to operate various ships' equipment, including the 20mm cannon, 40mm cannons, and so on. Most interesting was frozen rifle range shooting, using the 1903-A3 Springfield and the M1 Garand.

One drill could be considered enjoyable by the recruits. It was to jump off a twenty foot platform into an Olympic sized pool—a heated pool! This drill was meant to simulate jumping off a sinking ship. When a boot jumped off and hit the water, he was to swim the width of the pool to where the D.I.'s stood. Domenick in his bravado way did not swim the width of the pool, but rather the full length, underwater. The D.I.'s watching began to panic. One or two of them jumped into the pool to go get Domenick, but lo and behold he surfaced at the far end of the pool. The D.I.'s were furious. Domenick would pay dearly for his stupid stunt. He was given ten hours of extra duty. While other boots were relaxing between 7 PM and 10 PM, Domenick was washing out the "G.I." garbage cans in the mess hall. However, all was not lost, as the senior D.I. entered into Domenick's records a compliment regarding his swimming ability. That compliment would prove to be a meaningful one.

Where did Domenick get his swimming abilities? When he was twelve, he and some older boys played at the dockside of the East River. The older boys knew how to swim, but Domenick did not. They forced him to dive into the river—and he learned how to swim the hard way. Currents in the East River could be unpredictable, and boys did drown. Domenick learned how to negotiate those currents. He loved to swim so much that he traveled to many a place to swim, including the Brooklyn Tech School and the Red Hook Pool. To get to Red Hook he had to hitch on the back of a trolley car and ride for eight miles. He and other boys would sneak in by climbing a very high fence. He swam at Coney Island, beyond the jetties. He even swam in the Rockaways in high, rough seas.

During testing for IQ, aptitude and interests, Domenick volunteered for submarine duty. All who served in the submarine service were volunteers. This was mandatory. He had to take another rigorous physical, pass the decompression chamber test, and was given a battery of psychological tests. Domenick passed all with no problems, and was placed on the submarine list along with three other boots. As with all things Navy, they were placed in alphabetical order, which put Domenick last on the list.

After graduating boot camp, and having a seven-day leave, the men were awaiting orders for assignment. It should be noted that they all were now "the men." They were no longer know-nothing kids, low life's, recruits or boots. In the O. G. U. (Out-Going Units), hundreds of men were bunked in a giant Quonset hut awaiting orders. Each day all would go to bulletin boards to see if their names were an assignment list. After two weeks, Domenick saw the names of the other three men were on the list, and they were scheduled for submarine school at New London, Connecticut. This sight devastated him, and so he requested to see the Executive Officer in charge. This was an unusual request as this was not normally done in the Navy.

Yet, Domenick's request was granted. He got a meeting with the XO. He stated his case and asked why he wasn't chosen. The XO replied that the submarine service only needed three men for the class at New London. Domenick, being the fourth man was being "scrubbed." After a few days Domenick was called into the Chief of personnel's office. Fearful that he had over-stepped his boundaries by seeing the XO, he did not know what to expect. Surprisingly, the chief was friendly and spoke to him like a buddy. In reviewing Domenick's records, the Chief noted that he had excelled in the swimming test, was very physical in his actions, had good endurance as was displayed when boxing in two "smokers" in boot camp, scored fairly well in written tests, and last but not least, had shown guts by asking to see the XO.

"Your D.I. in boot camp remarked that you would be a good candidate for the U.D.T. Would you be interested in volunteering for U.D.T training?"

"Excuse me, Sir, but what is U.D.T.?"

"Underwater Demolition Team. It is an elite outfit." The Chief explained that U.D.T. men were trained to clear the way for beachheads before any invasions could take place. They act as reconnaissance to check which beaches might be best for landing troops and heavy equipment, map out terrains, clear obstacles by planting explosive charges just before invasions. They also took on many other dangerous missions.

To Domenick, this sounded even more exciting than submarine service, especially since he loved to swim.

"The training is tough. Usually only one-third of every class graduate. The rest "wash-out" for either physical or psychological reasons."

Domenick accepted this challenge. He was assigned to go to the Amphibious Base in Fort Pierce, Florida.

2 YEARS OLD

16 YEARS OLD

SIX - Frogman

Days at the U.D.T. training center began at 0500 (5:00 A. M.) and ended at 2200 Hours (10:00 P. M.). The trainees were called "pollywogs." Pollywogs ran wherever they went. No one walked. There was PT (Physical Training) before breakfast, and a four mile run on the beach after breakfast. Then more PT. After lunch the pollywogs "enjoyed" a three mile swim in the ocean.

A dangerous incident occurred during one of those off-shore swims, one which made Domenick and Jim Locksey blood brothers for life. A dark gray Bull Shark, approximately eight feet in length, glided through the water, trailing the men. When the men stopped to take a routine rest, and to pace themselves, this shark began circling them. Seeing the large shark fin circling, the men froze — and the circles got tighter. Suddenly the shark honed in on Domenick and brushed him in passing. It is said that when a shark brushes its prey, it will attack on the next pass.

Domenick became petrified. Seeing his buddy in trouble, Locksey began to frantically splash the water. This drew the shark's attention away from Domenick and it turned. But a miracle happened. The shark swam past Locksey without attacking, and it swam away, out to sea. Only God could know why, and perhaps He was with them that day. The men, stunned at first, cheered and hugged each other.

Then more PT! Also, they went to map class, recon classes, oceanographic studies, geographic studies, weapons familiarization, judo classes, Re-breather training, ditch and recovery techniques, use of demolition charges, and stealth techniques. Then more PT!

The DI's pushed each man to his limit. The philosophy was that any man can do ten times more than he thinks he can. When totally spent and unable to go on, they did "one more."

Endurance and teamwork was the paramount goal. "Ten times!" was repeated over and over. Discipline was demanded. The DI's were charged with getting the weak to "wash out."

At a weapons course range, they had four Marine Corps instructors teaching them the use of the .45 caliber Thompson sub-machinegun. Thirty-three men sat on the ground listening

attentively to an instructor explain the correct sight picture when aiming the gun. One pollywog appeared to have his eyes closed. A second Marine instructor singled out the unfortunate trainee and had him stand at attention in front of the group.

"Do you smoke, pollywog?!"

"Yes sir!"

The Marine sergeant told him to light up a cigarette, which he did, of course. Another Marine sergeant put a metal bucket over his head and ordered him to sing "Smoke Gets in Your Eyes" while continuing to smoke. As the hapless trainee tried to sing and smoke, this sergeant repeatedly struck the bucket with his "swagger stick." Needless to say, the pollywog soon passed out. When he came to, he returned to his place in the ranks. No one closed their eyes or even moved a muscle when the Marines gave instructions. Both the DI's and the Marines had a free hand in their methods. It is to be remembered that they only wanted the best to succeed.

The last week of training was called "Hell Week." The pollywogs were constantly on the move, continually harassed, controlled explosions in the water while swimming, awakened in the middle of the night by explosions, very little sleep or food, and other unmentionable techniques. Of the thirty-three men in Domenick's class, only eleven completed the course and graduated.

Only one-third of the class made it. Domenick was one of them. In his mind, this was the greatest achievement that could be accomplished, to really belong to a worthwhile "Gang." To become a full-fledged Frogman was the ultimate challenge the United States Navy had to offer. And, through the years, to present day S.E.A.L.'s, only one-third of the pollywogs complete the course.

After graduation, Domenick was sent to the naval Station at Little Creek, Virginia, for advanced Explosive Ordinance Disposal training. Following that, he received orders to join an E.O.D. Unit being sent to Normandy, France. Naturally, Domenick questioned why they were going to Normandy. The big invasion occurred ten months earlier. Why was U.D.T. needed?

Their mission was to either deactivate or explode underwater mines that the Germans had saturated the coastline of France. The German had planted more than five million mines. A great many were chained ten to fifteen feet underwater and someone or teams were needed to detonate them. These mines posed a great threat to shipping and the likes between Cherbourg and La Havre. While stationed in Normandy on the U. S. S. Olympia, Domenick and the U.D.T. team of fifty men worked very cautiously to detonate the submerged mines. The men worked in pairs and were taken over detected mines in a L.C.V.P. (Landing Craft Vehicle Personnel). The pair would dive and attach their satchel charges to the horned mines and then retreat to a safe zone before detonation. Many mines were cleared in this fashion, and it became a routine chore.

The horror of diving these mines was not only the possibility of making a mistake and being blown up, but also of finding half-decomposed bodies hung up on the chains or the mines themselves. Many Soldiers and Sailors were killed during the Invasion and their bodies drifted onto the mines. Whenever possible, Domenick and his teammates recovered web gear, rifles, and items which might help identify the dead. These images haunted Domenick for the rest of his life.

The team became very close in their relationship. They ate, slept, and worked together. Their closeness was as brothers, because that is exactly what they now were. Liberty on shore was usually wild, and each liberty had its own story. In the seaport of Portsmouth,

England, was jovial. They were very much welcomed. Food and drinks were very cheap and sometimes free. Everyone used to sing songs such as, "The White Cliffs of Dover," "Bless Them All," and some American Pop songs. Domenick loved to chime in as he had always loved to sing, especially on the beach at Coney Island. In France, a liberty to a small town was very solemn. This was probably because the German occupation forces had been very brutal to the French people. Also, many French had been killed as a result of the Normandy Invasion. The Frogmen were welcomed always, but in a quiet way. For whatever reason, Paris was declared off-limits for the team.

Clearing the submerged mines, three feet in diameter with horned fuses, became routine. Seeing them explode and produce a geyser of water rising twenty feet into the air, the Frogmen felt the vibrations from their safe zones, an exhilarating experience. To expedite the process of clearing so many mines, they experimented with blowing up two mines simultaneously. This was done successfully many times. However, nothing is always one-hundred percent perfect.

One day the two-mine routine was assigned to Jack "Tex" Farley and Mike Albanese on one team, and Jim Locksey and Domenick another. The two mines were approximately one hundred and fifty yards apart. While the men were in the water attaching their satchel charges, a mishap occurred. For whatever reason the first mine exploded prematurely. Farley and Albanese were blown into oblivion. The concussion from the explosion literally lifted Locksey and Domenick into the air and back down into churning whirlpools of water.

Both were pulled underwater. Disoriented, with deafness, blurred vision, and body trauma, the two men were near drowning. They tried to grope for the surface while struggling to hold their breath, their lungs on fire for the need of air. During this horrible space of time what went through Domenick's mind was that he was going to be joining the dead Soldiers and Sailors off the coast of Normandy.

Other Frogmen came to their rescue, and by the Grace of God managed to lift them up and safely aboard. Domenick could not see Locksey, or much of anything else.

"Is Locksey okay?! We got to get Locksey! Is he okay?!"

"Locksey's all right!"

Both men were taken aboard the Olympia and given injections to calm them down, plus x-rays and other examinations. Both men were given support by their fellow Frogmen.

"You guys had a tough time," said the team leader. "Thank your lucky stars that the concussion didn't set off the mine you were working on."

It was rough to be blown out of the water and almost drowned. But the loss of two teammates was even more to hard to take. This experience left emotional scars on both men.

To further examine both Locksey and Domenick, they were shipped back to the States to the Anacostia Receiving Station in Washington, D. C. Both men were bunked at the Receiving Station and periodically went for medical tests at the U. S. Naval Hospital at Bethesda, Maryland. Locksey was left with some loss of hearing in both ears, a slight visual problem in one eye, and possibly some nerve damage. Domenick was not so bad, as he had his left ear slightly impaired and possibly some nerve damage. The very stringent U.D.T. training had given each man a strong body to withstand the trauma of this horrendous explosion. But, the physical and emotional problems will, in future years haunt these two Frogmen.

In August of 1945, Domenick's parents, with the help of authorities, traced him to the Navy. The Navy then knew that Domenick had enlisted when he was sixteen. This was an embarrassment as they had not checked his enlistment papers thoroughly. He was sent home on medical leave.

His parents were so elated to have him home, and proud of his accomplishments, that they did not berate or try to punish him. Now they realized the worth of their son, and they treated him with love and respect. To appease his parents, Domenick promised to spend his time at home. He would return to the Navy after the holidays. He did get a job at Drake's Bakery, as a general helper, working the ovens, and loading trucks. The work was a snap for him, and the factory was only six blocks from his home. To keep in tip top shape, he rejoined the Bedford YMCA. Three times each week, Domenick would pass by Vickie's house. Plus, he occasionally visited his Uncle Sal. But he never saw Vickie.

As time passed, Domenick and his parents developed a fairly good relationship. Their holidays were very happy, especially since his sister, brother, grandparents, aunt and uncle were always there for festivities. During Christmas week, Domenick took his sister and brother to Fort Greene Park, prospect Park Zoo, and to Manhattan to see radio City Music Hall. He knew that he had to leave them in January. It could be a long time before he saw them again.

January came fast, Domenick went to visit his Uncle Sal and Aunt Angie. While there he boldly rang the Nigro's doorbell. Vickie's mother, Josephine, answered the bell.

"I'm leaving again soon for the Navy, Mrs. Nigro. I would like your permission to write Vickie."

"Why yes, of course, Domenick, you may write to her."

He wanted to see Vickie desperately, but he knew that he must follow the tradition of respect. It appeared to be working.

After seeing all of his relatives one more time, Domenick departed for Washington, D. C. Upon arriving at the Receiving Station, who did he meet? None other than his buddy, Locksey, who was working in a galley as a baker.

After hugging each other and talking a while, Domenick asked, "How did you end up being a baker?"

"The war is basically over. The U.D.T. has reduced in size dramatically. I decided to stay here in Washington, and I saw an opening for a baker. Bakers work in the galley, you know? So we eat good food and we get plenty of liberty. I "struck" for the job and got it. I was lucky I talked my way into it."

"All right. So what do you do on liberty in this city?"

"Domenick! Liberty here is the best in the world. There are thirty women to every man. And these women here are bold."

One day Locksey was looking through a newspaper and he saw that Stan Kenton, a renowned bandleader, was appearing at the Gaiety Theater. He knew that Domenick liked Kenton's style of music, plus there was a main feature movie shown after Kenton's performances. He went to his friend and suggested that they both go to the Gaiety.

Domenick was excited and he thanked Locksey for thinking of him. That evening they went to the show. During the movie, he noticed that a girl, sitting a few aisles away, was looking at him. He stared at her, and she stared back. With that she got up and went to the rest room. Domenick followed and waited for her outside.

When she came out he asked for her name.

"My name is Dorthea. Dorthea Cooke. Everybody calls me Dottie."

"My name is Domenick, but some call me Nicky."

"Hello Nicky."

"Would you like to go have a drink?"

"I don't drink alcohol. But I like ice cream sodas."

With that, Domenick went back and told Locksey what had happened.

"I'll see you back at the base," his friend said, smiling.

Dottie also went back to tell her girlfriend. So Dottie and Domenick went to the nearest Ice Cream parlor on Ninth Street N. W, They talked a great deal. It appeared that their chemistry was just right.

"Why were you staring at me?" He asked her.

"I like what I see. You tend to stare at me too."

"You have a beautiful face. I like your hazel eyes and blondish hair."

Dottie was twenty-one, five feet and five inches tall, and had the body of a ballerina. Domenick learned that she was one of the lead dancers at the China Royal Casino. Although the casino was Chinese in its decorations, it was a nightclub frequented by the elite of Washington, D. C. Dottie performed in at least two shows three times a week. Her manager, Franklin Gerry, was a good promoter. He could have gotten Dottie a great number of "gigs' on the road, but she did not like to travel. She was happy doing local shows.

Domenick and Dottie became very close from the moment they had met. They saw each other frequently, and he attended many of her performances at the Casino. In fact he got to know many people at the club, and he was well received by everyone.

Domenick's stay at the Receiving Station was boring—but liberty was good. In the day, he hung around the Station waiting for an assignment. At night, he and Locksey would have a ball.

One day Domenick saw a poster advertising that Lionel Hampton was performing at the Washington ballroom. He was excited and asked Dottie to go with him to see and hear the performance.

"I can't go there, Nicky. The Ballroom is segregated. It is only for Negroes."

Domenick being from New York City and raised with Colored People, Hispanics, Asians, and Jews, was surprised at her words. "There's no such thing as "segregation. People have to live together."

"Washington is below the Mason-Dixon Line. It is in the South. Here, there *is* segregation."

Poor ignorant Domenick could not believe that the nation's capital could have segregation in 1946. He told Dottie that if she didn't want to go, then he would go alone. He really didn't want to go alone. Being a lone wolf was not his way. So he asked Locksey to go with him. But Locksey could not make that show because he was on duty. Refusing to be discouraged, Domenick asked another friend named Johnny Weciano, a Corpsman from Jersey City, New Jersey. Johnny was happy to go along.

When both Sailors arrived at the cashier's window at the Washington Ballroom, a Colored woman looked at them, surprised.

"Are you sure you White boys want to go into *this* ballroom? You know this ballroom is supposed to be for Colored people only."

Domenick replied, "Where we come from there is no difference between people. So give us two tickets."

The young woman smiled and sold these Sailor boys from the North two tickets.

Domenick said to Johnny, "I guess Dottie was right, and maybe we got a lot to learn. By the way, Johnny, what is the Mason Dixon Line?"

The two Sailors entered the ballroom, which had approximately six hundred Black men and women inside, and everyone was dancing their feet off.

Johnny said, "Let's move as close to the bandstand as we can and get close to that exit door."

As they moved around the crowd, all eyes seemed to be on them. When they got to one side of the bandstand, a large Black man approached them.

"Get ready to fight and haul ass, Johnny," warned Domenick.

"What's wrong with you two guys?" asked the Black man.

Domenick snapped back. "Nothing. What's wrong with you, man?"

With that, the Black man said, "Whoa! You got me wrong. I'm not looking for trouble. I just want to know why you guys aren't dancing."

"Well, we don't know who to ask. We don't want to step into anyone's territory."

The big man proceeded to introduce the Sailors to two light-skinned Colored girls. Johnny started to dance, and he was a terrific dancer. Domenick did not know how to dance but he tried to fake it. While the two White boys were on the dance floor, Lionel Hampton, who was leading the band, saw then and did a double take.

The bandleader yelled, "Hey boys, what ya'll doin' here?"

Domenick yelled back. "I'm from Brooklyn."

"And I'm from Jersey City," yelled Johnny.

Hampton came down off the bandstand and shook their hands plus hugged them. After some small talk, he said to a waiter, "Anything these boys want is on the house." Lionel Hampton then hugged both of them and went back on stage.

The two White Sailors were treated like royalty. They were even given an 8" x 10" photo of the two Sailors and Lionel Hampton pictured together. It was a night never to be forgotten.

1946

Domenick   Lionel Hampton   Johnny

10

One night Domenick had a close call, when a woman tried to stab him.

There was a Sailor named Tino, who resembled Domenick so closely that he could have been his twin. Tino was a first class petty officer who was in charge of the galley. He had two ships sunk under him, and he had a number of psychological problems. When sober he was a gem of a guy. But when drunk he got extremely argumentative and violent. His attitude was that any problem could be solved by saying, "Piss on it."

One night Domenick was going off base on liberty. As he passed the guard gate and walked towards the road, a woman darted out and tried to stab him with a hunting knife. The U.D.T. Frogman side stepped her and quickly disarmed her. He dragged her to the gate guard and brought her under the flood light. It was revealed that she was pregnant, and, that she thought Domenick was Tino. She stated that the resemblance between the two was amazing. She continually apologized for attacking him. She said that Tino was avoiding her because she had made her pregnant. Domenick told her that if he saw Tino he would try to get him to talk to her. However, he knew that Tino's attitude would mean trouble.

As it happened, less than a week later, Tino got drunk and into such a rage that he ran completely through a closed screen door. Next he crashed through a guard rail of a second floor stairway, and hit the concrete sidewalk that it knocked him unconscious. An ambulance took Tino to the Bethesda Naval Hospital.

Domenick never heard anything about what happened to him.

When Domenick had first arrived at the Receiving Station, he had written a postal card to Vickie, signing it, "Your admirer." She in turn wrote a letter back to him, signing it, "With love." This started a series of romantic letters. Whenever he got a seventy-two hour Pass, Domenick would take a train home. When home, he dated Vickie, and they would visit his relatives and go to movies. Never did they even hold hands. When he had to return to the base, she accompanied him to Grand Central Station. There, everyone was kissing their girlfriends or wives goodbye—Sailors, Soldiers, and Marines. But Vickie, being the type of girl she was, only held out her hand and shook Domenick's hand. This confused him to no end. The confusing part was her letters were so romantic, yet in person she remained so distant. Since Domenick had been raised to respect the wishes of a girl, he learned to live with this relationship because he loved her so dearly.

It was amazing that their backgrounds were so alike. His mother's parents had come from Casa Buono, Calabria, Italy. So did Vickie's mother's parents. Domenick's father's parents came from San Demetria, Calabria. So did Vickie's father's parents come from that town. Both sets of parents had gone to P. S. 157 Elementary School, and, both attended St. Lucy Church. They knew each other's relatives. Domenick and Vickie had so much in common. And yet, even though she lived five blocks from him, in the same building as his Uncle Sal, it wasn't until he went to Norwood, New Jersey that he met her. Domenick was certain that it was ordained in heaven that he should marry this girl. If he needed kisses there were other types of girls to provide them. So, whenever he got a seventy-two hour Pass, he went to Brooklyn to see his relatives—and to be with his girl, Vickie.

On one of his liberties, Domenick took a day to go downtown to Navy Street. When he walked into the pool room where the Navy Street Boys hung out, all of the guys there were dumbfounded. Here was Domenick in his navy uniform shouting, "Hey guys! It's good to see you all!" The surprised men welcomed him with open arms. To them he was an all right kid. They had wondered what happened to him. Domenick told them why he joined the Navy, and he related his many experiences. They all admired him, but thought he was nuts.

His visit with old friends was short lived. They all heard a burst of gunfire outside. All of the men ran to a store front window and saw a car speed away. Across the street a man stumbled down a front door stoop, fell to the ground quivering, and died. As the police immediately arrived, all hell broke loose. They began questioning people outside. The "Bulls," detectives, burst into the pool room and lined all of the men against a wall. They began roughing the men up while they questioned them. When they saw Domenick in his uniform, they told him to beat it and never come back. Domenick thanked the detectives and quickly got out of there. What happened at the pool room was never known as the Navy Frogman never did go back.

Domenick Scarlato, Ed.D

SEVEN - Seamen Honor Guards

As Domenick hung around the Receiving Station awaiting orders, a Chief Boatswain mate approached him.

"I understand that you are a U.D.T. man."

"You bet. Is there any assignment for me?"

The Chief said, "No, but I have a good deal for you if you would volunteer. You must volunteer for this job."

"What is this supposedly good deal you want me to volunteer for?" Domenick asked, with a good deal of skepticism.

"To belong to the Seaman Honor Guard."

The Chief explained that the Seaman Honor Guard was a highly respected unit because they stand guard at the Tomb of the Unknown Soldier. They also attend ceremonies for dignitaries and act as a burial detail at Arlington Cemetery.

"They only work nine to Five, and they have weekends off."

This sounded good to Domenick and he accepted the assignment.

At that time the service used a Soldier, a Sailor, and a Marine to guard the Tomb. Over the years this would change, and it now only the Army that stands watch. To perform his duties at the Tomb and the Arlington Cemetery, Domenick had to practice with his fellow

Guardsmen on a daily basis. They had to be the sharpest looking men in the service, a challenge which Domenick loved.

One day while standing in formation, a deuce-and-a-half truck backed up and hit Domenick with its rear wheel, knocking him to the ground. In the process the wheel went over his right foot. Everyone yelled for the driver to stop the truck. Good thing it did. If the truck had not stopped it would have run over him. He was taken to Bethesda Naval Hospital to be treated. Luckily, x-rays showed no broken bones, only contusions and lacerations. He was lucky that the ground had been dirt rather than concrete, or he might have lost his foot. His ankle and foot were bandaged and he was sent to the Receiving Station with crutches.

After three weeks on the crutches, he went to sick bay and complained that when he walked he felt something protruding underneath his right foot. The Corpsman told him that he was developing a callous. After more visits for the same complaint, the Corpsman asked a doctor to look at Domenick's foot. The doctor, an Ensign, looked at the foot from about two feet away and said that it was a Plantar Wart. "Cut it off," he told the Corpsman, who cut away the callous. Even though Domenick continued to feel pain and complain to the corpsman, the Ensign doctor's diagnosis was etched in stone. This problem would plague the Sailor and Frogman for years to come.

What was not known is that at the Naval Hospital they had not x-rayed his whole foot, just the ankle. If they had looked at the foot they would have seen dislocated and crushed metatarsal heads and falange, and, a small bone protruding at the bottom of his foot. They had performed an incomplete x-ray battery, and the sick bay doctor had completely misdiagnosed the metatarsal head. Domenick was not a wimp who complained too much. He learned to live with the pain. In the service anyone who went to sick bay too often was considered a malingerer, and only a wimp constantly complains. This injury will plague him for years to come.

Washington, D. C. had "thirty women to a man" at the closing of WWII. Liberty for a Sailor was like paradise. Or, so it would seem. But in reality, most guys sought one woman, and so it was with Domenick. His "one' was Dorthea "Dottie" Cooke, professional dancer.

As a little boy, Domenick loved to sing. As a teenager, he would sing for himself or for anyone else who would listen. He sang while working, and on the beach at Coney Island. Some said that he sounded like Perry Como, others said, Frank Sinatra or Dick Haynes. Domenick insisted that he sang in his own voice and his own style. He didn't want to copy anyone. Dottie told him that his singing is what made her fall in love with him. She wanted him to audition for her manager, Franklin Gerry. Domenick, in some things, was basically shy and modest, but she finally convinced him to sing at one of her rehearsals at the China Royal Casino.

He sang three songs: "Long Ago and far Away," "All or Nothing at All," and "I've Got You Under My Skin."

Franklin was impressed, and even more so when he learned that Domenick had never had a single music or singing lesson.

"With a little stage training, and the right guidance, you could go right to the top — and maybe be a star." The manager handed the Sailor his card. "When you get out of the Navy, look me up. I'll take care of you. Don't waste natural talent. Not many men are born with such a talent. You're lucky."

Franklin later stressed to Dottie for Domenick to contact him.

"Yes, Franklin, I will do my best." Dottie was very happy about Domenick's new found prospects of entering show business.

It is too bad that this opportunity for a singing career was lost, as an unfortunate incident happened after Domenick was honorably discharged from the Navy. One day his mother overheard him talking to his brother about how he could be able to travel all around the U. S. A., and be able to visit his shipmates while pursuing his singing career. Domenick showed his brother Franklin Gerry's card, and also his small address book with all of his shipmates' names and addresses.

"They have all invited me to visit. It might happen if I can get started in Washington, D. C.

Upon hearing this, Domenick's mother decided to destroy this address book. When no one was around that is exactly what she did. She later had the nerve to tell him what she had done.

"You are home now and may get married soon. You should be working and saving money instead of trying to go gallivanting around the world."

Domenick was so furious he could have killed. Then again, it was his mother, so what could he do? He left the apartment and stayed out all night to collect his thoughts.

"Piss and punk" — what a vulgar term. Domenick learned about that term, and about the injustice it brings.

It was a hot summer night and early morning. At 3:00 A.M. most of the bunks were humming with hard breathing and occasional snores. A Chief Boatswain came in drunk as a skunk and fumbled through the darkness looking for his bunk. He mistakenly crawled into Domenick's bunk, with Domenick in it, sleeping. The U.D.T. Frogman thought they were being attacked. He rolled out and began pulverizing the Chief. The commotion woke all of the others, and someone turned on the lights, somewhat fortunately for the Chief. Domenick realized who he was, not an enemy.

The Chief was taken to sick bay to be patched up. It was natural that Domenick was placed under arrest, by order of the Officer of the Deck, for striking a superior. He went before the captain with a Summary Court martial hanging over his head, which could bring six months in Portsmouth Naval Prison and a bad Conduct

Discharge. Domenick explained what happened and his story was verified by over twenty men who had been present that night. The Captain reduced the Summary Court Martial charge, but stated that he had no choice but to reduce it to Deck Court Martial. This was to appease the Chief, who sustained two broken teeth, a broken nose, and a dislocated jaw. Domenick received thirty days "Piss and punk" time in the Receiving Station Brig. This brig was operated by the Marines, and, as anyone knew, the Marines had no love for Sailors. Piss and punk meant bread and water and every third day a prisoner was given a meal. Sleeping was done on a spring, with one blanket. Luckily it was summer. It must be remembered that this type of justice was muster before the *Uniform Code of Military Justice* was adopted. It is unnecessary here to relate the emotional and physical ordeal which Domenick experienced, but it was sufficient for him to vow that he would never go to a jail again. When he was released from the brig, he returned to duty and was treated like a celebrity. Everyone knew that he had gotten a raw deal, but they saw that he took it all in stride.

Domenick's tour with the Seamen Honor Guard was very fulfilling. He was always elated when he stood his watch at the Tomb of the Unknown Soldier. And, he never minded performing in parades or ceremonies. However, to go to Arlington to bury Sailors or Marines was for him too much of an emotional experience. After burying a seventeen year old Sailor, Domenick said to himself that this was his last one. To see the parents, relatives, and many a young girl crying at the Chapel, during the slow march, and especially at the grave site, was too much to bear. Not only did Domenick get tears in his eyes, but so did all of the men in the firing squad. When that burial detail got back to the barracks, Domenick went to his Chief.

"I can't take this burial detail anymore. I'm tough enough to cut a man's heart out, but when it comes to family I'm a softie. Relieve me from the burial detail and I will be happy to do the rest of my duties plus clean the rifles, or whatever you want me to do."

"You have to do it all or get a transfer."

"Well, Chief, I hate to say this but I'll take the transfer to wherever it is."

To this day, whenever Domenick hears "Taps" he gets tears in his eyes.

Domenick Scarlato, Ed.D

EIGHT - Destroyers

Domenick was transferred to the U. S. S. Everett F. Larsen, which at the time was docked at Newport, R.I. The destroyer was named after a Marine who had been killed on Guadalcanal and had received the Navy Cross. Domenick traveled to Newport with two other Sailors. He was placed in charge of John Krell and James Gardener since he had held the rate of Seaman First Class the longest. Krell and Domenick became close buddies.

Within a week's time the Larsen, the Hanson, Thomas, and Goodrich, sailed for the North Atlantic. Why? No one knew. As any Sailor would declare, the North Atlantic was always rough waters. The squadron of destroyers experienced a terrific storm. Anyone who went topside had to wear a life jacket and a safety-line belt. The sea produced waves so high that they covered the Bridge. Most of the men were seasick, some of them too sick to perform their duties. Therefore those who did not get sick had to perform extra duty. The Hanson had one Sailor washed overboard. The Larsen was called to help search for the lost Sailor. Everyone knew that the search was futile, but search they must. After two days, The Hanson and Larsen rejoined the other two destroyers.

The seas were somewhat calm then, and sailing became fairly routine again. Where young men live in close quarters there will always be confrontations. There were always be bullies who wanted to rule the roost. Domenick, new to the ship, was a prime target to be picked on. A radioman named James Brown looked for an excuse to pick a fight with him. Domenick was placed in charge of a detail to move furniture and equipment out of the Radio Shack. Brown had a magazine in his hand and asked if anyone wanted to look at it. Domenick said, "Yeah," and reached out for it. Brown looked him straight in the eye and threw the magazine into a garbage pail. Domenick ignored this. Next, Brown pushed a chair hard into him. The challenge was accepted and the two men went at each other hot and heavy. Brown went down hard, and the other men yelled that he had had enough. The crew picked up Brown and set him into a chair. They placed a cool, wet rag over his face. Domenick was cool, and he combed his hair and relaxed against the bulkhead. The radio Officer stepped into the compartment and saw Brown's battered face.

"What happened here?"

Brown said, "I fell down the ladder, sir."

The officer looked around the room and stared at Brown. "Did you hit every single rung on your way down?"

No one spoke.

"Go to sick bay and get taken care of."

Brown and the officer departed.

"It's about time somebody straightened brown out," said a Radioman.

Domenick gained some respect for Brown for not squealing to the officer. The next day, while he was on the fantail, Brown approached him. *Here we go again.* But brown extended his right hand to shake as he apologized. This went round the ship like wildfire. No one would challenge Domenick again. Everyone became his buddy.

Through the grapevine, Domenick heard that the Engineer Division needed a man. So he went to the Chief Engineer, who was a Mustang (former enlisted non-com) who had risen to the rank of Lt. Commander. He requested to be transferred from the Deck Force to Engineers.

"What makes you qualified for this position, Scarlato?"

"I can read a micrometer, and, I'm willing to learn whatever it takes to be a Machinist, sir."

The Chief removed a micrometer from his desk and also pulled out a piece of his hair. "Take a reading."

Domenick measured the hair and stated that it was .003th of an inch. The Chief verified that he was correct. With that, the Chief gave Domenick an Engineering manual.

"Study this. In three months, you must pass the test for Fireman First Class."

"Sir, shouldn't I pass the test for Fireman 2nd Class?"

"No can do, Scarlato. You are a Seaman First Class. You cannot go backwards, unless you are demoted. It's against Navy regulations. It has to be a lateral move. This is a tough assignment. Do you really think you can do it?"

"I will do it, sir."

"All right then. I'll talk to the XO about getting you in."

Two days later Domenick was assigned to Engineering Division. He began serving his watches in the engine room, and his workday was in the "A" Repair Gang. He was the only Seaman on the destroyer working in Engineering. He studied hard, asked a lot of questions, got help from fellow crewmen. Three months later he passed the test for Fireman First Class.

The ship conducted war-time maneuvers in the Caribbean Sea. Domenick's battle station was Damage

Control Party. The crew worked four hours on, and four hours off around the clock. In war-time scheduling, General Quarters (Battle Stations) were called all hours of the day or night. Even though a crew member may have worked or been on alert all night, and was off duty during the day, he could not go to his rack to sleep. Crew Quarters were closed during the day for clean-up. Many of the crew tried to catch up their sleep in gun turrets, whale boats, or wherever they could find a niche.

Relieved of their watch, Domenick and Krell were dead tired. Since they couldn't go to Quarters to get some sleep, they looked elsewhere to "crap out," as the Sailors used to say. They located an opportunity under a table in the crew's Mess Hall. This table was situated up against the bulkhead and kept them partially hidden from sight.

The squadron of destroyers were scheduled to tie-up along side each other in what was called a "nest formation." The Larsen, Goodrich, Thomas, and Hanson prepared to execute the maneuvers to anchor and tie-up. As per the plan, Goodrich anchored first. Next the Hanson came along side, anchored, and tied to Goodrich. Then it was the Hanson's turn to tie up to the Larsen. As the Hanson came along side, she came in too fast and collided with the Larsen. The collision was so violent that it damaged the Larsen's guard rails and part of the superstructure. The entire crew turned out in case the ship was in jeopardy. When the Damage Control Party went to the Mess Hall to check for damage, they saw Domenick and Krell lying under the mess hall table. Since the Hanson had hit this side of their ship, they feared that the two men had been badly injured or killed. They immediately called for a medical Corpsman. But they approached the two men lying there and touched them. Both men jumped up, startling everyone. Damage Control seamen could not believe their eyes, because they could not believe that the two had slept through the collision which had happened on this side of the Larsen. The Captain ordered the Corpsman to examine both men anyway. The two Sailors were found to be physically okay, but they were clearly fatigued.

One positive thing resulted from this incident. The squadron came off the four-on, four-off, plus a work day, and returned to the normal four-on, eight-off plus a work day. Meanwhile, although Domenick and Krell might have gotten some credit for the scheduling change, the embarrassed pair found it difficult to live down the incident. Wherever they went on the ship, they were called the "Big Sleep."

The squadron of destroyers headed back to the States, escorting CVA-41 Midway carrier. Their destination: Brooklyn Navy Yard for overhaul. Arrived in June of 1947. Domenick could not believe he could be so lucky. His home, his family, and his girlfriend, were only one mile from the Yard. He didn't write to tell anyone. He wanted to surprise them — and surprised they were!

When he came to their door at 177 Classon Avenue, his mother and father cried, his sister and brother jumped for joy, and his Aunt Angie passed out. Aunt Angie was famous for passing out when she got excited. For her this was normal. His Uncle Frank hugged him. After much talk and a great Italian meal, Domenick said it was time for him to visit Vickie. At 1032 Bedford Avenue, he rang the door bell with three dots and a dash—"V" for victory. Vickie came to the door and screamed with joy. This time Domenick wasted no time. He grabbed her and kissed her. Everyone in Vickie's house was glad to see him. Her mother, Josephine, her father, Frank, her 10 year old sister, Theresa, and her 20 year old brother, Benjamin were happy. Best of all, his ship was to undergo a major overhaul, which could take up to six weeks. Liberty could be had every other night—hopefully.

During the crossing of the Atlantic, Krell and Domenick became close friends. Each spoke often about their past childhood and Navy experiences. Krell confided that he was from Niagara Falls, married and waiting for a divorce. He was five feet six inches tall, husky, with a good sense of humor. His behavior was at times a little weird, but Domenick figured that the War may have influenced his actions. He had served on a submarine, where he screwed up and caused a compartment to flood. For that he was busted from First Class petty Officer to a Fireman Second Class. Now he was on the Larsen to finish out his enlistment. Domenick told Krell how he had screwed up, although not his fault, and did thirty days "piss and punk" in the brig. Krell stated that he liked to drink good liquor. Domenick explained that he did not care for liquor because of a childhood experience.

Everyone can relate to their first drunken stupor. Domenick's experiences and his stories were always unique. His moment with "the devil's brew" occurred when he was ten years old. His father was working nights, and his mother, brother, and sister were not at home. For Domenick to be alone was a rare occurrence. When he was alone, he would always talk to or play with his imaginary friend, "Jim." When alone in the playground, he played handball with Jim. He hit the ball, and then Jim would hit the ball, each taking turns. Domenick was always fair as to who would hit the ball and who would miss. Sometimes Jim won. Domenick was a good student in school, but he often got in trouble for talking to his neighbor. At least, he was the one who always got caught. One time Domenick got caught talking, and the teacher placed him in the girl's section of the classroom with the hope of embarrassing him. Domenick got caught talking to the girls. This disturbed the teacher's lesson, so she isolated him in a cloak closet. After a time she heard voices coming from the closet. Upon opening the slide door, there was Domenick talking to his imaginary friend, Jim. The teacher gave up and told him to take his regular seat. By this time it was well known that to Domenick, Jim was real.

That evening alone at his home, Domenick started to play cowboys. He set up two chairs for horses, and he and Jim rode the plains looking for buffalo. After a hard ride, they sashayed up to the bar for a drink. Now it was well known that his mother made good homemade liqueurs from 100% alcohol. Her products came in colors: red bottle, blue bottle, green, and yellow bottles. Domenick went to the closet and took out the red bottle and two shot glasses. He poured a drink for himself and one for Jim. Of course, he drank both shots. After a few rounds he began to get dizzy, so he put away the bottle and shot glasses. Then he collapsed on the floor and threw up all of the liqueur. When his family came home, his mother saw him lying on the floor in a pool of red liqueur. She thought he was bleeding to death. She screamed so loud that her sister, Angelina, who lived in the apartment below, raced up the stairs. After examining Domenick, Aunt Angie said, "He is not sick, he is drunk. That's your red liqueur. Don't you smell the alcohol?" His mother went into a rage and began hitting and kicking Domenick until her sister stopped her. After his mother regained her composure, she sighed in relief and lovingly cleaned Domenick up to put him in bed.

He woke up the next morning with many aches and pains.

"Momma, what happened to me? My head hurts and I have bruises."

"That is what happens when you drink liquor. The liquor gives you headaches, and mothers give you bruises."

Domenick said, "I guess Jim got away."

While the Larsen birthed at the Brooklyn Navy Yard, Domenick invited some of his shipmates to his home for nice Sunday Italian dinners. The first two to be invited were Krell and Farrell, who was from Kansas City. The guys were elated to be treated so well. Of course the 'chow" was out of this world. Both were very impressed with Vickie, and told Domenick that he was a lucky guy. The second two invited were Benson, from Georgia, and Clark, from Texas. This proved to be comical as his mother and Vickie could not get used to the different accents, one from the deep south, the other from the southwest. Domenick had to act as an interpreter. It must be remembered that at this time the areas of the country were still far apart in terms of accents and traditions.

Although most of his liberties were spent with Vickie and/or family, he did save time to be with his shipmates. On one such liberty, Domenick and Krell went to Times Square. While walking around 42nd Street they picked up two girls. Krell went off with a redhead named Virginia. Domenick, in good conscience, soon left the girl and headed back to the ship. On the subway, a Spanish speaking gentleman approached him and asked for directions. Domenick gathered that he was Cuban. Through some Italian words and sign language, it became clear that the man was lost. His name was Jose Citron, and he wanted to get to Times Square and the club, Havana Madrid. It was almost impossible for Domenick to adequately give directions. Being the good Samaritan that he was, Domenick went out of his way to escort the man to the Havana Madrid club. Jose was so happy that he hugged Domenick and gave him his card.

And he gestured, inviting the Sailor to come back someday to visit the club. Domenick kept the card, figuring that the man worked there. Maybe he would come back.

The next morning at breakfast, Krell couldn't wait to tell Domenick that he was in love with Virginia.

"One night with a broad and you are in love. Are you wacky?"

"I want to marry her!"

"Are you out of your mind?! You are twenty-five years old and where are your senses? You are not even divorced yet."

Here were two buddies who could say anything to each other without offending. Domenick tried everything short of hitting Krell to knock some sense into him, but it was useless. Fortunately the ship was scheduled to go on a "Shakedown Cruise" to test all of the work that was done to her. They would go to Norfolk, VA, and then onto the Caribbean, and Guantanamo Bay, Cuba.

The squadron of destroyers arrived at Norfolk Naval Base in September of 1947. Liberty here in this little town was as expected. To the Sailors and Marines, the city was called "Shit City." Norfolk city was filled with bars, honkytonks, and whore houses. Some of the bars welcomed Sailors with open arms. Others had signs which read, "No Sailors or Dogs allowed." Domenick never believed in paying for sex, and he had been indoctrinated effectively at Boot Camp about the horrors of venereal diseases. However, after being on board the ship for such a long time, plus pressure from shipmates, Domenick agreed to go to a whore house with them.

When he went into a room with a fairly pretty girl, she said, "It will cost you ten dollars."

"I only have two dollars."

After looking him over, the girl agreed to accept only two dollars. As Domenick was taking off his neckerchief, a Madam entered the room and asked the girl for the ten dollars.

"I only have two dollars," the girl replied.

The Madam was out raged and yelled at the girl, even slapping her very hard.

Domenick snapped, "You lay off her! She was only trying to be nice."

Then the Madam took a swing at him, but he grabbed her arm and gave her a good smack, knocking her to the floor. As the woman began screaming, Domenick left the room. In the hallway he saw Krell sitting in a chair, and Farrell just coming out of one of the rooms. At the end of the hallway was a very large man who had a blackjack in his hand. The Sailors froze for a second. Domenick knew he had to do something quickly. Even though there were three Sailors against one very big guy, other men could be in the building, with weapons. Domenick put one hand behind his back as if to grip a pistol under his blouse.

"Man, if you want a hole in you then come ahead. If not, please step aside."

Fortunately the ploy worked, and he did step aside. The three Sailors quickly left the building.

A short while later Domenick became more "pissed off."

"I've got to get even with those rats. I'm going to call the cops on them."

Farrell said, "That sounds like a good idea, but in this corrupt city, who's going to believe a Sailor."

"They might believe you if you were a Navy officer, Dom," suggested Krell.

"Okay, I'll try it. What have we got to lose?"

Domenick called the police and pretended to be Lt. Commander Cahill from the destroyer squadron.

"…It is a disgrace that my men and other military personnel are permitted to go into that house of ill repute. Shouldn't you go and clean that despicable place out?"

Domenick and his shipmates were soon amazed that this gimmick worked. In less than ten minutes, a paddy wagon with cops pulled up in front of the whore house. The establishment got cleaned out. The three Sailors went on their merry way. Domenick never went to a whore house again.

Norfolk was a crazy town, but Krell was even crazier. He constantly talked about Virginia and how much he loved her. He "jumped ship" and went A.W.O.L. to New York City. Fortunately he returned within five days, just before the Larsen got underway for maneuvers. Krell was given a Deck Court Martial and received a $200.00 fine, plus 100 hours of extra duty. He couldn't be put into the brig because destroyers did not have a brig. And, the Larsen needed every man available. Domenick was nearly speechless because of his friend's actions. He did offer some consolation, but he felt that Krell was "cracking up."

During maneuvers, Domenick was again assigned to the Damage Control Party. His battle station was up forward under the 5" x 38 gun #1 turret. Ordered to retrieve a pump, he opened the hatch just as the Twin 5" guns blasted broadside of him. The concussion of the cannons caused the metal hatch door to hit Domenick back into the compartment, knocking him senseless. After a few minutes he came to but was deaf with a high pitched ringing in both ears.

Someone screwed up, because before firing the cannons, a warning is announced to tell the crew above decks to clear the area. Obviously, Damage Control personnel did not get the message over their headphones. The one positive note was that were it not for the hatch door acting as a shield, Domenick could have been fried. The ringing in his ears lasted for about a week. His hearing seemed okay, but in later years it would affect him.

The squadron pulled into Guantanamo Naval Station for liberty. Liberty at "Gitmo" was good. A launch boat took them to a terminal. Then an old train took them for a slow ride through jungles to Camero City. During the train ride, it shocked and depressed the Sailors to see the thatched-roof houses on stilts and half-naked people, using dug-out canoes. This was beautiful Cuba as advertised in pamphlets from Havana? Little half-naked boys ran alongside the train, yelling for chocolate, cigarettes, or tee-shirts. It was a heart-breaking sight.

In Camero City, streets were dirt roads with hitching posts for horses. Four federal policemen rode into the city and tied their horses in front of a building set on concrete blocks five feet off the ground. Most of the shabby buildings were elevated because of floods in rainy season. Bars had swinging doors like the ones in old USA westerns. The beer, called *Yatui*, was strong.

The women were loose. These loose women would give lots of pleasure for a dollar bill, or even a man's tee-shirt. The confusing thing to Domenick was to see a Crucifix hanging from their necks. It seemed that the more he saw of the world the more confusing it became.

As the squadron headed back to the States, Krell and Domenick were cooling themselves one day, just outside a manhole from the engine room. Lt. Commander Cahill, executive officer of the Larsen, approached and ordered the men to attention. He began to chastise Krell.

"Why are you wearing a ripped shirt on deck, Sailor?"

Domenick knew that Krell was still under tremendous pressure, and saw his friend's hands begin to tremble. So he attempted to explain the XO that they had just popped up from the hot engine room for some air. But all of a sudden Krell ripped off his shirt and threw it at the XO. Luckily it missed and went overboard.

Krell screamed, "You wanted the [blank blank] shirt. Now take the belt!"

He removed his belt and threw it too at the executive officer. Again, luckily it went over the side.

Lt. Commander Cahill said, "I can't deal with this man."

And he quickly departed.

It wasn't long before Krell's name was called on the P.A. system. The announcement ordered him to report to the quarter deck. There he was placed under arrest and confined to his bunk. Upon arriving at Key West, Krell was escorted off the ship under guard. The crew was told that Krell would undergo psychological evaluation. Domenick was devastated. He loved Krell like a brother. As it happened, he never did learn anything about Krell's fate.

While in Key West, Domenick's enlistment time was up, so he and two other Sailors were assigned to go to Jacksonville Naval Air Station to be discharged. The Greyhound bus ride to Jax was long and tiring. Traveling along U.S. 1, a two-lane highway, there was nothing but shacks in small towns, except for Miami and West Palm Beach. Jacksonville, Florida, was a large city, and across from the Greyhound Bus Terminal was a bar called, "The South's Oldest Bar."

"It sure looks like it," said one of the Sailors, and all agreed.

Next the three were taken by a Navy bus to Jacksonville Naval Air Station and were bunked in a massive aviation hangar. Three thousand men bunked there, all waiting to be discharged. It took three weeks for Domenick and his two bus-mates to be processed and separated with an Honorable Discharge.

While they waited to be processed, many men slept in parked airplanes—to avoid work details—and enjoyed liberty at night. Florida weather in November was nice and warm. Liberty was great. But Domenick couldn't wait to get home. Finally he boarded another Greyhound bus bound for New York City. This trip took forever. When he arrived in Manhattan, it was 6 A.M. on Sunday morning. He hailed a cab and told the cabby that if he could get him to 177 Classon Avenue, Brooklyn, by 6:30, he would get a $5.00 tip. That was big money in those days. The cab arrived at Domenick's house at 6:28.

Everyone was awakened and there were joyous screams. Aunt Angie passed out, as usual.

Domenick Scarlato, Ed.D

U.S.S. E.F. LARSON DD830

1947

Domenick Scarlato, Ed.D

NINE - Civilian Life

November of 1947 was a beautiful time of the year. Domenick was discharged from the Navy, and he was with his family and girlfriend. He could now see Vickie as many times as he wished. This was also a time for servicemen everywhere to settle down and adjust to civilian life. Adjusting was difficult for many veterans. In fact, the government issued to each man being discharged a booklet entitled, "Going Back to Civilian Life," in the hope that it would help keep veterans out of trouble and give guidance for re-entering civilian society. It took Domenick quite a while to adjust: He had some difficulty communicating with men who had not served in the military. His patience was limited, and people who were self-centered, braggarts, and, the slow or just plain ignorant, distressed him to no end. To make matters worse, jobs were scarce as there were suddenly millions of veterans looking for work. No one needed Domenick's skills in demolition or his underwater skills. Even his machinist knowledge was of little help since many old time machinists were out of work, because many defense factories and shipyards were laying off men in large numbers.

Domenick wanted to work in order to save money to get married and possibly buy a house. He was willing to work at any job, whether it be labor or whatever. Under the G. I. Bill of Rights, he was eligible to receive twenty dollars a week if he could not find a job. So he went to the employment office to apply for this benefit. Naturally the lines at the employment office were very long, and the clerks who handled applications and claims were very cold, rough, and snobbish. They had a bad attitude and treated people like cattle. It was a demeaning environment for veterans, or for anyone else. After standing in line for an hour, he was given an application. He waited another hour. When he finally reached a clerk to file his application, the clerk scolded Domenick for not completing the application in full. He proceeded to enter the item which he had missed, but the clerk loudly told him to go back to the end of the line. Words were passed between Domenick and the clerk. A security guard came over and sided with the clerk. He went to the back of the line. After God knows how long, he filed the application and was told to have a seat in a special section to await an interview. After waiting for two hours, Domenick's nerves were tingling. He approached an individual behind a desk and inquired how much longer did he have to wait. This individual, in a stern voice, told Domenick to go back and sit down and wait for his turn. Domenick moved his seat up front so he could observe the operations of this office. After a long time, he noticed that when a clerk brought over new applications they were dropped onto the top of the pile. He realized now why his turn was taking so long. His application was at or near the bottom, and it wasn't climbing. Domenick got up and started looking through the pile to find his application.

A clerk grabbed his arm and pulled him away from the applications.

Domenick kept his cool and tried to tell the clerk what he had observed. The clerk acted like he was God Almighty, so Domenick picked him up and threw him over the desk. The security guard, plus a police officer, took him into custody and walked him outside. It was a good thing that both of those men were veterans and understood how Domenick felt. They told him that ninety percent of the people working in the employment office were not veterans. They had no compassion and acted like little Caesars. Give small people authority and it goes to their heads. The security officer advised him to go downtown to the main office and keep his cool.

Adjusting to civilian life came hard. Many veterans re-enlisted in the service because they just did not fit into society. Domenick thought about going back into the Navy, but his love for his family, and for Vickie, kept him home. Adjustment was demanded, and adjust he would.

He finally landed a job with the Rockwood Chocolate Factory, six blocks from his home, as a laborer. To do this job only required a strong back as it required unloading one-hundred pound sacks of cocoa beans. There was no "Hi-Lo" to unload the trucks. A line of men carried the sacks from the truck to conveyor belts. At the end of the day, you were very tired and you looked like a chocolate man from the powder on the sacks. At least Rockwood had showers for the men to use before they went home.

Domenick was a good worker and ambitious. In one season he moved from the loading dock to the production line, where girls boxed the chocolate products. He made sure that the girls never ran out of boxes. By the second season he had moved from the production line to becoming a "Temper." A Temper constantly checks the temperature of the cooking chocolate. He also regulates the sizes of products, as well as generally monitoring the operations of the production line. This wasn't the best job in the world, but it gave him a salary so he could save for his coming marriage.

An interesting thing happened on the 4th of July, when Domenick took Vickie to Manhattan to see a movie and a stage show at the New York Paramount Theater. Harry James was playing at the paramount. Following the movie and show, Vickie and Domenick were walking along Broadway when he spotted the Havana Madrid Night Club. He related the story about how he had helped a Cuban man named Jose Citron.

"Jose asked me to come visit the club sometime. What do you think? Want to go inside?"

"Okay. I guess it wouldn't hurt to go inside and see if your friend is still here."

So they did. The club was beautifully decorated like tropical paradise. They went to the bar and ordered a drink. A band was playing, but club rules dictated that unless you sat at a table you couldn't dance. Domenick asked the bartender if he knew Jose Citron, and did he work here.

The bartender laughed and said in a heavy Spanish accent, "Senor Citron is the *Patron*. He owns this club."

This surprised Domenick and impressed Vickie.

"...How is it that you know Senor Citron?" the bartender asked.

And so Domenick told him the story about meeting Jose on the train and escorting him to back to Manhattan. At which point the bartender called over the cigarette girl and told her to call Senor Citron.

When Jose came out and saw Domenick, he cheered in Spanish and came over and hugged the former Sailor.

"It *ees* good to see you, *mi* young Navy amigo!"

Jose could now speak a fair amount of English, not good, but good enough to communicate. Domenick introduced Vickie as his girlfriend.

Jose invited them over to a table, where they chatted for a while, and the *Patron* ordered a round of drinks. Jose asked if Domenick wanted a job. And for some reason, the club owner asked him if he could sing.

"Yes, I do sing a little."

"You will sing for me now, Domenick, my friend. Right now, please."

The former Navy Frogman was a little embarrassed but he sand a song called, "Besame Mucho."

"Hey! You are very good singer. With a *leetle* training and some Spanish, you could sing in our band."

Domenick was excited about this surprising opportunity.

"I will think it over, Jose. I must discuss this with my girl. Maybe we will be getting married,"

Jose looked at Vickie. "*Theese ees* a good opportunity for Domenick. And, maybe you both can take a trip to Havana in the winter. I have another very *fantastico* club there also."

Vickie did not say anything about this offer.

"Thank you, Jose, for your very kind offer. I will let you know," Domenick stated sincerely.

The couple stayed for a while and enjoyed the club. The bill they got was peanuts compared to what they drank.

When they got home, Vickie spoke about Jose's offer.

"It's a great opportunity, but what about our marriage? What about your plans for night school?"

It appeared that Vickie was not to keen on Domenick working in a nightclub. For a second time, it also appeared that another chance at show business was going to pass by.

According to tradition, the wedding was paid for by the girl's parents. The boy was obligated to furnish an apartment. At the time Vickie and Domenick got officially engaged, a relative of the Nigros promised them an apartment in the building he owned. This was at a time when all the veterans coming home were not only seeking jobs but also getting married. Apartments were as scarce as hen's teeth. This relative's promise was a God send, However as the saying went, "All is not well in Brooklyn." Vickie's brother, Benny, had made his girlfriend pregnant.

This girl wanted a quick but formal wedding, with all the bells and whistles. She even walked down the aisle of the church in a white virgin gown. Vickie's parents paid for the wedding as an appeasement to the pregnant girl. All of this threw a wrench into Vickie's and Domenick's wedding plans.

Now Domenick had to pay not only for the furnishings of an apartment, but also for the rings, the wedding, the cars, flowers, reception hall — everything! Both sides had many relatives and friends, and all expected to be invited to the wedding. There would be over four hundred guests. It appeared that the wedding was going to be like a circus. To pour more gasoline on the fire, the nice relative who promised Vickie an apartment reneged. He probably got more money from the rent and also got "paid under the table," as a bribe was called in the business world. If Vickie and Domenick were to marry, they would have to move into the "coal water" five room apartment with his parents, brother, and sister. Why would this be necessary? Benny and his bride moved in with his parents. And, as it has been stated, apartments in 1948 were as scarce as hen's teeth due to fifteen million veterans coming home.

This put a second thought into Domenick's head about getting married.

Many thoughts passed through his mind as to what his future should be. Although he loved being home with his family and his girl, his adjustment to civilian life was difficult. He was only twenty years old and restless. Everywhere he went he encountered tensions.

Some of this was due to the difficulty of communicating with men who did not serve in the military. His run-in with the insensitive, arrogant people at the Employment Office was only one example of how veterans were treated. Another time he overheard, in a bar, three men talking about the War. One said to another, "Too bad the War didn't last another year. I could have paid off my mortgage on my house with the money I was making." This infuriated Domenick and he tried to control himself, but a surge ran through his body and all hell broke loose. When the smoke cleared, so to speak, one man was knocked out, a second was laid out atop a table with a blackened eye. The third man backed off and just stared petrified. As Domenick knew most of the men in the bar, they covered for him. Domenick thought, *Is this what our servicemen and women fought and died for? The "Almighty Dollar" for these rejects?* It is coincidental that years later Domenick heard a similar conversation by two men in the Brooklyn Navy Yard. On this occasion, a Welding Apprentice named Hank Cespedes, a Marine veteran, knocked out the man making a similar statement.

Domenick loved his mother and father very much. But the family traditions called for a young man to settle down, get a job—no matter what it is as long as it is honest work—and get married. That was the most important thing. Now there was the pressure of planning a wedding, with his mother's "Help."

Domenick tried to talk to his father for some guidance and help. The only thing he got from his father, "I don't want to get involved. Let the women handle everything." Domenick felt trapped as a prisoner to family traditions. His upcoming wedding was becoming a nightmare, a circus, and far from being a joy.

Domenick wanted to travel, to see the U.S.A., and to visit his shipmates who said they would put him up. He would only need train fare. But that plan had been trampled when his mother destroyed his address book. The possibilities of going into show business were only fading dreams.

A slave to traditions and family values, a veteran faced with scarce opportunities, people who disrespected veterans, and a young man who wanted to enjoy the rest of his life,

Domenick needed to make a decision. There were four roads for him to choose from.

Should he go back into the Navy? He had passed his 3rd Class Petty officer's exam just before being Honorably Discharged. He could be on the ladder to becoming a Chief petty Officer. In the military, Domenick would only be responsible to the United States Navy and its missions.

Could he follow "The yellow Brick Road" to fame? He had opportunities to become a famous singer. Could he go back to the China Royal Casino, to Dottie and Franklin Gerry/ Or, he could accept the offer from Jose Citron, *Patron* of the Havana Madrid Night Club. In show business, Domenick would have to work late hours, do many rehearsals, and possibly be required to travel where his manager booked him. He would work to please audiences, nothing more.

The third road was the "Bliss of Marriage." His responsibility, growing each day, would be to support a family. He would be a prisoner of family traditions and values. He would be a slave to the high tech world of the Industrial Complex. Maybe his only choices were to either work in a factory or for the Department of Sanitation, as did his father, uncles, and future father-in-law. At best, he could apply for other Civil Service jobs.

Last, and certainly least, he could take the road downtown to Navy Street and live the fast life with people who believed, "It's a sin to pay for anything."

Which road did Domenick take? Did love triumph and family traditions rule? Or, did the young and free man choose a different road?

That my friends, is another story.

Made in the USA
Middletown, DE
23 September 2020

20401059R00071